Twayne's United States Authors Series

Sylvia E. Bowman, *Editor*

INDIANA UNIVERSITY

PAUL GREEN

PAUL GREEN

VINCENT S. KENNY

Marymount College

 **186**

Twayne Publishers, Inc.   : :   New York

Barry College Library
Miami, Florida

Copyright © 1971 by Twayne Publishers, Inc.
All Rights Reserved

Library of Congress Catalog Card Number: 79-125254

MANUFACTURED IN THE UNITED STATES OF AMERICA

To a Full House:
Gloria, Stack, Brian, Maeve, Maura

Preface

THE PLAYS and movie scripts of Paul Green have been seen by more men, women, and children than have all the works of Arthur Miller and Edward Albee. Green is rare among playwrights alive today: aside from the merits of individual works, his contribution to the symphonic drama as a new art form alone guarantees him a place in the development of American culture. In addition, as early as the 1920's he called for an indigenous Negro theater, a concern that outraged his fellow Southerners but which helped pave the way for the emergence of the professional Negro today, both as actor in dignified roles and as spokesman for his cultural heritage. He is a member of the National Institute of Arts and Letters, an authority on folklore—American and international—a Library of Congress consultant, and holder of countless awards of distinction. But with all of the hundreds of thousands who have flocked to the spectacular dramatic events in the great amphitheaters at Roanoke, Williamsburg, Bardstown, St. Augustine, and many other cities; with all of the forty-odd scripts written for George Arliss, Will Rogers, Lionel Barrymore, Clark Gable, and other famous actors of Hollywood; with the numerous plays and stories on the black man written with the authentic Negro touch, Paul Green's name, paradoxically, is virtually unknown today. For example, there has not been published a single, complete study of the man or his works, except for a profile written by his friend at the University of North Carolina, Agatha Boyd Adams. Scholars are quick to point out that writers in every age suffer a reversal as new vogues set in. But in this case, the reversal persists at the same time that even greater numbers of people travel great distances to see Green's plays.

One possible reason for Green's failure to attract a wider collection of critics and professional scholars can be accounted for in his outright rejection of the commercial theater, after long, bitter experience with it; and in his assumption that the future of American theater lies only in outdoor drama. In numerous essays and lectures, he has indicated that symphonic drama constitutes the strongest possibility for the American theater to achieve distinction.

A second reason for his obscurity lies in the subject matter that Green has worked with over the years. Like Walt Whitman, he fuses the common man, the outdoors, and America into a mystical, but working, democracy. These are not popular themes, nor is there a viable spirit in the modern theater which has sprung from existential pessimism. World War II dimmed whatever hopes for progress of the human spirit the more sanguine political philosophers had described. God was dead, as were the possibilities for a man to stretch himself out in heroic lengths. The antihero, the statistically average man, Robert Musil's "man without quality," like C. P. Snow's organization man, sum up an age that has no time for romantic dreams of greatness. Green's voice, therefore, sounds to the sophisticate as out of a past hardly remembered, carrying a message signifying nothing. His demand of all men of all ages to grow in spirit, to renew the epical struggle of the heroes of the past in the building of a free and equitable world, ignores the fact of human placement in a limited and absurd universe. If judged by modern views of man Green's continuing epical assaults and human triumphs in his symphonic dramas have the aura of a "Miniver Cheevy," and add nothing to his stature as a serious artist.

But the fact that millions have seen Green's symphonic dramas suggests that the playwright's abiding faith in human nature and his belief in the present and in the future contain a truth not to be expunged, and also indicates that many share Green's idea of a theater and an abiding optimism that echoes the words of Saint-Exupery: "To be a man, is to feel that one shares in the building of the world." Early or late in his career, this quotation could express Green's compassionate hopes for humanity and his sensitive concern for man who must experience broken dreams and promises. Green, a realist, confronts the destructive presence of evil as well as the infinite and mysterious possibilities of human perfection. In the same way that Whitman alludes to the "trippers" who mock his cosmic confidence, Green consciously persists in this unfashionable, "simplistic" assessment of human virtue, as he forms a cultural expression from the memories and aspirations of America.

There is no intention in this book to present Paul Green, the man; perhaps his life and writing will be the subject for future studies. But here the work itself will be examined, with

Preface

very little concern for the biographical facts bearing upon the writing. The material is inviting for Green was a prolific writer to the extent that the library at the University of North Carolina contains a vast file of unpublished material: sketches, stories, and comments that Green never intends to refashion. His vast published work, however, fits into three fairly well-defined categories, although all of them ultimately come down to a literature of the folk. The first two classifications include his concern with the bitter lot of the white tenant farmer and the plight of the black man in his fight with the soil and society. These works were written out of the author's own memories of his work in the fields with the whites and the blacks. Green approached the subjects through one-act plays, dramas, novels, short stories, and numerous essays that comment on the fictional work. For purposes of clarity, the two categories will be examined hereafter in this study as distinct aspects of white and black folk-literature, even though Green wrote them concurrently, from 1919 through 1937. The third grouping falls more obviously into separate discussion, for with the first symphonic drama in 1937, with a few exceptions, Green devoted his writing energies exclusively to that specific form of expression. In all three sections of my examination, chronology will give way to the more logical inquiry into the major themes explored by the author.

My gratitude must be expressed to Paul Green, a patient, wise, and gentle man. I suspect that he has never said "no" to any request from anyone. My best wishes, too, to Professor Robert Schuman of Duke University, who graciously pushed me beyond the talking stage with his practical advice. I was assisted immeasurably by the librarians at Marymount College and by my friend Marian Downey who, I suspect, must take some responsibility for this book. Mrs. Evelyn Gottfried surely must be the best secretary in America since she was able to translate my words into typed sense. But my clearest dependence was, as ever, on my wife, Gloria, editor, consoler, and suggester. All of this attests to Paul Green's insistence that the work of any man rests on the joint efforts of all, although final accountability reverts to the spokesman.

VINCENT S. KENNY

Marymount College

Contents

Preface

Chronology

Part I. LITERATURE OF THE FOLK

   1. The Land—More of an Enemy Than a Friend   1
   2. Rebels with a Cause   12
   3. The Tyranny of Family and Tradition   24
   4. Black or White—It's All the Same   39
   5. Three Black Lamentations: Abe, The Hymn, and Bigger Thomas   59

Part II. SYMPHONIC DRAMA

   6. Experiments in a New Form   77
   7. Lost and Found—A New World Dream   92
   8. Additional European Explorations   107
   9. Laying the Foundation of America   120
   10. The Shaking of the Foundation   130
   11. New Areas for Exploration   141
   12. Conclusion   147

Notes and References   152

Selected Bibliography   157

Index   163

Chronology

1894 Paul Eliot Green born (March 17) in Lillington, North Carolina, son of William Archibald and his second wife, Betty Byrd Green.

1914 After graduation from Buies Creek Academy, serves as Principal of the country school in Olive Branch, specifically to earn money for expenses at the university. Also earns money as a sandlot, ambidextrous pitcher.

1917 Under Norman Foerster's direction, his first play, *Surrender to the Enemy*, wins prize for best one-act play at Chapel Hill. At the end of freshman year, enlists in the army. Before going overseas, publishes at own expense collection of poems, *Trifles of Thought*.

1919 After twenty-five months, resigns from the Corps of Engineers as a 2nd Lieutenant. Saw service at the front for one year in Belgium and France.

1920 Five one-act plays written and produced by The Carolina Playmakers at Chapel Hill.

1921 Graduation from university. Lasting influence of professors there: Norman Foerster, James Holly Hanford, Edwin Greenlaw, Horace Williams, and Frederick Koch.

1922
1923 Kenan Philosophy Fellowship subsidizes two-year graduate study of philosophy at Cornell University.

1922 Marries Elizabeth Lay, daughter of the Reverend George Lay, rector at St. Mary's College in Raleigh. Elizabeth another promising author in the Playmakers.

1922
1936 Teaches in Philosophy department at Chapel Hill; occasional leaves of absence to write for Hollywood and radio.

1924 *Salvation on a String*, a collection of short stories.

1925 *The Lord's Will and Other Carolina Plays*. One-act play, *The No 'Count Boy*, wins the New York City Belasco Cup, his first notice outside regional theater. Edits *The Reviewer*, a monthly journal of the arts at Chapel Hill.

1926 Summer residence at the MacDowell Colony, New Hampshire. Publishes *Lonesome Road: Six Plays for the Negro Theater*. *In Abraham's Bosom*, his first full drama, produced in New York City.

1927 Wins Pulitzer Prize for *In Abraham's Bosom*. *The Field God* produced in New York City. Publishes *The Field God* and *In Abraham's Bosom*.
1928 A Guggenheim Fellowship, extended for a second year,
1930 allows a study of theater in Germany and England.
1928 *In the Valley and Other Carolina Plays*.
1931 Completes his first music drama, *Potter's Field: A Symphonic Play of the Negro People*. *The House of Connelly* produced by the Group Theater in New York City. Publishes *The House of Connelly and Other Plays*.
1932 Sporadic work in Hollywood for Warner Brothers, Fox,
1936 Paramount, and other companies.
1932 *The Laughing Pioneer*, the first of his two novels.
1934 *Roll, Sweet Chariot*, an adaptation of *Potter's Field*, produced in New York City. *The Enchanted Maze*, a satire of university life, produced at Chapel Hill.
1935 *This Body the Earth*, second novel. A full play, *Shroud My Body Down*, produced at Chapel Hill.
1936 *Johnny Johnson*, with music by Kurt Weill, produced by the Group Theater in New York City. Publishes one-act play, *Hymn to the Rising Sun*. Leaves philosophy department at Chapel Hill for a new department of dramatic arts, under Frederick Koch, also at Chapel Hill.
1937 *The Lost Colony*, produced at Roanoke Island and continues to present day. Turning point of career; emphasis hereafter on symphonic drama.
1938 *The Southern Cross*, a one-act play on outmoded Southern attitudes.
1939 *Out of the South*, a collection of six complete plays and nine one-act plays, all published before. First book to win national reputation. Produces second symphonic play, *The Highland Call*, at Fayetteville, North Carolina.
1940 President of the National Folk Theater Conference.
1942
1941 Collaborates with Richard Wright for Broadway production of *Native Son*. Elected to the National Institute of Arts and Letters. Writes *A Start in Life*, a one-act play for radio.
1942 Renews sporadic career in Hollywood; buys house in Santa Monica.
1943 *The Hawthorne Tree*, a collection of essays on education

Chronology

and the human spirit.
- 1945 *Forever Growing,* a second volume of essays on education and humanism.
- 1947 Produces his third symphonic drama, *The Common Glory,* continuing to present day at Williamsburg, Virginia.
- 1949 *Dog on the Son,* a collection of old and new short stories.
- 1950 Member of Executive Commission, United States Nation-
- 1952 al Committee for UNESCO. Visiting lecturer to Asia for Rockefeller Foundation and UNESCO.
- 1950 Produces symphonic drama on George Washington, in nation's capital, *Faith of Our Fathers.*
- 1951 United States delegate to UNESCO, General Conference in Paris. Adapts Ibsen's *Peer Gynt* for Group Theater in New York City.
- 1953 *Dramatic Heritage,* the first of three collections of random essays on the theater and the world. *The 17th Star,* a pageant for Ohio's sesquicentennial, opens for a two-week run.
- 1954 Adapts Bizet's *Carmen* for Central City Opera Festival in Colorado.
- 1955 *Wilderness Road,* symphonic drama produced by Berea College in Kentucky.
- 1957 *The Founders,* symphonic drama, produced in Williamsburg, Virginia, to commemorate the founding of Jamestown.
- 1958 *Drama and the Weather,* second collection of essays on the theater. A seventh symphonic drama, *The Confederacy,* opens in Virginia Beach, Virginia, for a two-year run.
- 1959 *Stephen Foster,* symphonic drama, opens in Bardstown, Kentucky; continues to present day. *Wings for to Fly,* three radio plays for the Negro theater.
- 1962 Guest of the Greek government in Athens for International Conference in the Performing Arts.
- 1963 *Five Plays of the South,* a collection of five revised plays, edited by John Gassner. *Plough and Furrow,* a third collection of essays on the theater and the world.
- 1964 Writes the screen version of John Howard Griffin's,

Black Like Me, for Film Features.
- 1965 Symphonic drama, *Cross and Sword*, to celebrate the founding of St. Augustine, Florida: continues to present time.
- 1966 Tenth Symphonic drama, *Texas*, in Canyon, Texas: continues to present time.
- 1968 *Words and Ways*: Stories and incidents from Green's Cape Fear Valley Folklore Collection. Published by the North Carolina Folklore Society.
- 1969 *Sing All A Green Willow*, a "Folk Fantasy Morality" written as a Fiftieth Anniversary gift for the Carolina Playmakers.
- 1970 *Trumpet in the Land*, symphonic drama, opens in Dover, Ohio, to celebrate the Moravian missions to the Indians in Ohio.
- 1971 *Home to My Valley*, a shorter version af a long-planned collection of Cape Fear Valley folklore.

PART I

LITERATURE OF THE FOLK

"And they dig and they sing.
O earth, give us answer.
Jesus, hear us."

CHAPTER *1*

The Land — More of an Enemy Than a Friend

A PROPER DISCUSSION of Paul Green and folk literature must begin with a passing reference to Frederick Koch, "Proff" to Green and all the other devoted drama students at the University of North Carolina. Even more than Horace Williams, philosophy professor at Chapel Hill, or James Campbell, a teacher at Buies Creek Academy, Koch inspired Green so that the young boy's life shifted to a religious involvement in art, one that remains unchanged to this day. "Inspired" is the correct term, for Koch's pedagogy eschewed dogma about the "well-made" play, historic perspective, and all the other Classical considerations of theater; it substituted the criteria of enthusiasm, spontaneity, accurate observation, and honesty. He brought to his students a respect for the folk play, for an art form which challenges the sensitive probing artist to achievements beyond the scope of commercial theater. Paul Green shared Koch's reverence for folk material, but he went far beyond the vision in the actual accomplishment of his plays. It is safe to say, however, that everything he wrote, including the later symphonic dramas, is, in Koch's terms, "earth-rooted in the life of our common humanity."

From Green's first published work in 1924, *Salvation on A String*, a collection of short stories, through his last novel, *This Body the Earth,* in 1935, Green developed three major themes, all of which revolve around the fact of man's suffering: nature's cruelty may turn a man bitter; it may cause a man to seek love and mutuality; it may turn a man to a real or a surface God and religion. These themes are less developed, however, than they are repeated or explored from a different perspective in each new work. Although a design was not consciously followed over the eleven years, the body of writings can be seen now as following a cycle in which the 1935 novel is consistent with the first plays written.

The view that Green presents is that of a man who works in the fields from sunup to sundown for a crop which can be washed out before harvest; or, if he has a good harvest, the prices are down while the mortgage interest is up. If he is lucky, he shares his burden with a wife and finds a mutuality with others in the same situation. He may turn for consolation or meaning to the ministers of a mysterious and vengeful God and shout "Amen," or he may laugh in scorn or defiance. But in whatever way he attempts to ease the burdens of his existence, inescapably the land draws him back with brand new hopes that experience cannot kill. Green found in the folk and their resiliency the rich material of Classical tragic choice and consequent catastrophe.

Like the Irish playwrights Green had discovered through Koch, he raised the seemingly prosaic subject matter to the level of universal art. Like them, he developed an overriding idea in his important work that encompassed the three themes— nature's hostility, God and religion as a panacea, love and mutuality—into a single one: the ultimate need and test of a man is to be able to stand independently alone or in harmony with his neighbors. Early or late, Green's preoccupation with this major concern in his life and art is obvious. In his writings, a pattern emerges, however, expressing a philosophy that shifted from a cynical view of human achievements to a regard for humanity that places him next to Walt Whitman. There are exceptions to this outline, but, in Green's work prior to 1937, the hero asserts his independence, achieves a minimum of self-satisfaction, and then succumbs to forces beyond him. This progression, which consistently displays Green's thinking during this early period, appears in any one of the three themes examined in a play or a story, or it develops from all three if they are explored at the same time. The final impression one receives is that all three notions ultimately merge into one: the awesome mystery of the universe and man's endless struggle to locate himself in it.

The Land—More of an Enemy Than a Friend

Following the publication of *Salvation*, ten stories of which appeared again in 1928 in a second collection, *Wide Fields*, Green published three collections of plays—*The Lord's Will and Other Carolina Plays*, in 1925; *Lonesome Road: Six Plays for the Negro Theater*, in 1926; *In the Valley and Other Carolina Plays*, in 1928—and separate editions of individual plays. Except for the radical difference of form, the three major themes as explored in all these stories, novels, and plays could form a single body of thought. Only after 1937 does Green clearly move away from this pessimism about man's futile struggle against nature; then he begins to see man not as the victim but as the shaper of history.

I Nature's Hostility

Green did not often explore exclusively the notion of nature's cruelty turning men bitter. For the most part, he had more confidence in a person's ability to conquer nature, even if he did not always express it. One poignant example of the futility of a farmer's grinding life can be found in an excerpt from an otherwise sanguine one-act play, *Saturday Night*, in which three old men muse on the passing of time. One of them figures his life in terms of miles walked. With sixty-five days out for plowing, he calculates he has walked five miles a day three hundred days of the year, or fifteen hundred miles a year. Not counting his boyhood, he concludes he's been walking like this for fifty years, for a total of seventy-five thousand miles. His cold statistics evoke a wistful commentary from one of the others: "About as far as to them stars. Wisht I'd done all my walking on a path going there." In this blend of the real and the metaphysical, Green presents the farmer's life, although he rarely finds these folk aware of the better path to the stars. The back-breaking hours defeat such dreams and limit values to the completion of chores and to simple physical relief.

Eddie York, in one of the *Salvation* short stories, "A Tempered Fellow," typifies the tenant farmer's bleak lot in which survival is a daily struggle against the land. In this story, Green isolates a single incident in the lives of two people which culminates their misery and describes a way of life shared by tens of thousands of others. Eddie's burning ambition to pay off the mortgage attaches him to his three acres of cotton, a mule, a cow, and the pigs, while his love dissolves even beyond his memory. His crazed murder of his wife bursts out of an animal nature which has supplanted his humanity. Green refuses to comment on Eddie, nor does he demand sympathy for him in the framing of the events. He merely observes that illiteracy, limited social intelligence, and an unbridled temper, added to the prolonged industry, leave Eddie a child at the mercy of his passions. The brutally hard work, coupled with a fierce love for the soil, conflict with his deep love of his wife, Ola, whose contrasting sensitive nature makes husband and wife strangers. Green indicates that such a combination of factors and personalities can lead only to destruction.

In all these works, Green sees young men come to the soil each year, confident in their strength, normally acquisitive, likable in their rugged independence. After a few years of drought and tempest, they are old men, sexually and spiritually impotent; they are men in name but hardly distinguishable from the mules they drive. He knows that the fault must lie with Eddie and the others like him, for environment cannot be the final control of life. On the other hand, he sees how the best intentions shrink away in the hoeing of crabgrass from tobacco rows, how beauty or any abstraction disappears in the dawn milking of cows. At some point in the endless drudgery the personality disintegrates or camouflages itself; and relationships—husband and wife, father and daughter, mother and son—turn to indifference or hate. Constitutionally unable to place the blame on determining factors outside the person, Green in these writings sadly wonders like Job over the mystery of suffering and of human endurance. Like Job, he has the facts of the riddle but no solutions.

Old Wash Lucas, one of Green's earliest one-act plays, dramatizes this same theme. Wash and his daughter, Ida, literally square off against each other with knives over a dispute involving his cash box. Ida—thirty, thin-chested, pasty-faced, and a typical farm slattern—keeps house for her father, an old miser whose avarice destroys Ida, her brother, and everyone else. The miserable situation only repeats a story experienced in thousands of households, a tyranny that leaves desirous young girls dried-up spinsters who are, ironically, bitter as a result of the charity they perform. Green suggests another side to Wash's case, one found in the old man's own brutal childhood. As a result of his early beatings, he lives in a jungle, with survival his only concern. In the relationship of the father and daughter, Green effects an overwhelming sense of entrapment, of the dead end of impoverishment; their lives, victimized by forces which destroy affection, encourage cruelty, and make the young old. In simple, terse, realistic dialogue, he traces the lives of primitive folk who have absolutely nowhere to go.

Green found that the woman in the house, like Ida and Ola, was the victim of the land to a greater degree than the man in the field. Society determines the man's dominant position, and the man himself more or less shapes his own life according to the demands of the farm. Initiation of a significant change rarely if ever falls to the woman: she serves, obeys, and echoes. In *Fixin's*, a play written by Green with his sister Irma, a woman tries to free herself by bringing into her cramped days some little beauty, "life's fixin's." When her demands to be treated as a person are ignored by her husband, she packs her bags and leaves; and she accomplishes in the rebellion one of the rare female assertions of freedom in Green's early writing.

The same poignancy appears in the short story, "Her Birthday," a poetic study of loneliness. Green sets the scene on a farm on an unbearably hot Sunday, the birthday of a nameless, forty-year-old spinster who minds her dying mother. Pulp romances and reverie fill out whatever life she has left over after the farm chores. On this special day, the woman, close to her change in life, hopes that Walter will drop by to say hello to her mother. She had gone with him for years until her mother's rejection of his social inferiority broke off the romance. Now Walter is married and has beautiful children who only emphasize her lost possibilities. Her daydreams become more frenzied as the day passes: now he will come not to greet her mother but to kiss her for her birthday. She hears a noise at the door, rushes to it, and finds an old hound. She goes to her wizened old mother and cries her heart out as the white, gnarled hand moves over her head in silent compassion. Her birthday ended, she awakens the next morning: "But the beauty of a dewey world and the resurgence of morning life stirred no flush in her dull eye. She stood beneath the ancient pediment and architrave of rotting glory and wept in unspeakable loneliness."

The formal language of this final line deepens the exquisite mood of solitude. Such words are usually reserved for the hero, or for events of great consequence. But this spinster is an unknown, the whole of her life shared by a senile old woman. Green underscores her sterility with the slight touch of the wasted erotic, or the longed-for erotic. She's in a wrapper, and her plump body is sweating just the way she would like Walter to find her. For a few nights running, she has dreamed of Walter, snakes, and foul odors in his hot kisses —an obvious mixture of phallic longing and Puritan revulsion. She gazes endlessly at the family portraits and remembers only the sensual stories she heard about them. Everyone—her decrepit mother, the relatives on the wall, Walter—all have known love, all except her. The reliable crutch of religion fails her, the magazine stories only awaken the longings that can't be satisfied, and she can find no reward for her dedication in attending her mother: she only wishes her dead. Like Ida, this frustrated character has nowhere to go.[1]

These people are beyond sorrow. The spinster flushes out unavailing daydreams on her birthday, Eddie reverts to an unknowing infant state after a bestial act of murder, and countless others evince this theme of bitterness. In the one-act play, *The Last of the Lowries,* the lost women, like their fictional cousins in Synge's *Riders to the Sea,* keen over the death of the last of their men. In the short story "Chair Endowed," a husband and wife engage in a continuous love-hate battle: now in combat, now in intercourse, but always in sorrow over their portion of existence. They only echo the complaints of the host of tenant farmers who are numbed from contact with the land. Those who come to the soil with bright hopes turn as hard as the clay they plough.

II. *Love and Mutuality*

These plays and stories, for all of their accurate observations and emotional intensity, focus on only one facet of human experience. Had Green limited his vision of man to an organism impersonally destroyed by nature, the deep compassion he manifests would be only a vulgar tag; the insistence later in his writing for the heroic response that brings about change would come from a poseur whose writings belong exclusively in the popular women's magazines. Green's agonizing over the destruction of all these young men and women, even as he presents them in their bleak surroundings, on the contrary, indicates that change is possible, that some amelioration is available. This second theme is muted when placed next to the larger one of the tenant farmer's vicious battle with nature; it nonetheless holds greater implication for Green: man's immense capacity for suffering and the pain itself suggest a transcendent quality that lifts him out of human degradation. It hints at the eternal pulse that man carries within him.

But Green does not portray his characters as haunted by the afterlife. The consolation that he himself takes from these burdened people is completely earthbound; it comes from their own created social harmony, from their inner convictions that result in tight relationships in the family and in society. This solidarity does not obviate the suffering, nor does it answer the questions that Job asked. Rather, it insists that man act upon his realization of the suffering and discover in the action the value of mortal interdebtedness and human intercourse. In working out this theme of alienation relieved, Green continued the earlier explorations of Hawthorne and Melville and paralleled the solutions found in Hardy and Conrad.

One of Green's finest one-act plays, *The Old Man of Edenton*, develops this idea of created relationship. Although the 1750 setting and the Gothic trappings remove the story from the usual folk milieu, the subject is consistent with this problem of suffering and amelioration. Three officers call on old Jules to execute an order for his arrest on the charge of placing a spell on the governor's daughter. A cannibal servant, a monstrous idol, and a steady wail somewhere in the house terrify the posse; but the men are determined to have Jules behind bars before the night is over. Jules is equally bent on letting them in on his secret: his wife has leprosy which she contracted in a far-away country. When she appears on the scene with her nose eaten away, her sightless eyesockets, and her one empty sleeve, the officers flee in horror. Without sentiment, Green offers a man weighted down by calamity, by a freak of nature, hooted at by an unchristian community, but constant in his love for a shadow of a woman.

The nobility of compassionate love can be matched by the intensity of young love as a positive and good way to confront life. Green presents this sudden bursting of love and its painful discovery in "The Cornshucking," a story in the *Salvation* collection with which very few readers will fail to identify. In it, the grueling work of picking the corn is only a factual background for the more important epiphany of love for the boy and girl. And in this proper setting of a community involvement the boy and girl discover each other. A man and a woman, loving each other and awarding that love to others, create a dignity for themselves and their neighbors that no debasing work can violate. The same tenderness and mutuality of community interest appear in *Saturday Night,* the one-act play already mentioned. In merely relating the conversation of three old men and in pointing to their vision, this play pulls the reader into the camaraderie of the old men. Using the "smiling aspects of life" and a single prosaic incident in the lives of unimportant folk, Green pictures the significant fumbling of human beings for happiness. He captures the emotion of young love's discovery and sudden manhood in a moment of fear that explodes at once into joy, blended with a contentment in the elders that "the old will go on and the young will go on." The notion that all will be well has particular meaning because of the earlier conversation in which one old man cited the bleak statistics on the number of miles a man clocks his life; but the miles are only the facts of the case. How a man walks them, or finds meaning beyond them, determines his worth. In these discoveries and relationships, Green finds humanity's reason for existence. The land imposes enormous loads on a man's back, but they are lightened by the harmony that family, community, mutual interests, compassion, and love bring.

In "The Sixth of June," one of the few harrowing tales in *Salvation on a String,* in which an old mad farmer searches for his wife, already dead for a week, Green tells of the power of love as a continuing reality in the face of suffering. Everything is hinted at in the story, just as tenderness hides in common things. The farmer, who awakens on his wedding anniversary and cooks breakfast as a treat for his wife, plans to take her shopping for the day. When he cannot find her, he searches for her throughout the house and in the fields

The Land—More of an Enemy Than a Friend

until he himself is found by the men from the asylum in the haystack where he had found his beloved Jennie dead. In this tight, almost clinical story, both themes on nature emerge: the constant battle with the crops, weather, insects, rats, and poverty and sickness probably killed Jennie and snapped the old man's mind, although the reader is never told. But, in the worst of situations like this one, the love of two people carries beyond death: it endures even in madness.

This mutual love holds together the four parts of "The Humble Ones," a short story in which the author sings a paean to love: "So they reaped and sang as the days went by. Morning, noon, and night they toiled in the vineyard of the Lord. Ceaselessly, they followed their star." The woes of the farmer and his wife, Ollie and Lettie, befall every man; but in this moving tale the problems are highlighted. Their son is stamped to death by a favorite horse; Lettie suffers migraine headaches and wanders off looking for their dead son; Ollie develops cancer and lingers in a painful death. In this profound, if at times depressing, account of mankind's frustrations and defeats, simple devotion to one another overcomes or minimizes all the disasters: a husband and wife transcend their humiliation because they have become "humbled before something unknown, something mightier than they."

III God and Religion

The third theme that recurs throughout these early works also concerns man's reaction to nature. In the setbacks that life provides, a man turns to God and or religion, for better or for worse: usually for worse when he shifts to God through religion, for invariably he worships an idol contrived by scheming ministers. Their pseudo-mystical communion with the other world depends on hysteria and allows the ministers to corrupt the gullible folk. In too many cases, their fiery zeal destroys their own families, whose ordinary rights are abnegated by the minister's "higher calling" to spread God's word. One such self-appointed spokesman in *The Lord's Will* refuses help to his wife Mary, who is burdened by a crushing poverty, and to his daughter Ruth, who is dying of pneumonia. He argues that God intended him not for work in the fields or the village mills, but for preaching "the word" to His folk. Convinced of

God's will operating through him, he allows Ruth to die. His action infuriates Green. Always the humanist, Green insists that one must be a man first before he is a server of God; that the minister is obliged to work on a pastoral level, with no radical dependence on supernatural help.

Green scored these abusive churchmen in another one-act play, *Unto Such Glory*. He was so exercised by the message of the plot that he wrote a long preface on the evils of "itinerant evangelists." Fortunately, his balanced humor prevailed; he changed the preface and play from what would have been only ineffective preachment. The result is a hilarious account of a minister who is justifiably tricked by a shrewd layman, one who could easily be placed among Chaucer's anticlerical characters.

Despite a real contempt for the pietistic, traditional religious approach to God, Green, in subsequent works, chose to ridicule it. He suggests in great belly laughs that all this ministerial mumbo-jumbo should not be taken seriously. In the title story of *Salvation on A String*, he tells of Zack Broadhurst, the worst pagan in Little Bethel County, whose near-conversion to the church was thwarted when his trousers fell to his ankles, "leaving him hanging there naked as a yard dog in the face of his neighbors."

Things of magnitude rest on the most trivial matters: Zack's salvation on a broken string, like Othello's ruination on a handkerchief. In another spoof of evangelism in the same collection, Green details the greatest revival in the history of Little Bethel in "The Devil's Instrument." In it, Tim Messer, a "heathen," finally capitulates when he goes to the mercy seat after his friend Sam had been converted by the irresistible Brother Baxter. Baxter starts in after Tim is seated and the church is rocking with his thundering words. One eighty-year-old crone beats Tim in the face; other women bare their breasts for general nursing. Tim finally confesses and collapses as the whole church rejoices. But fortunately, like Zack, Sam and Tim backslide to their old sinning, normal selves again.

The Rabelaisian laugh that echoes throughout this period of writing is invariably in connection with orthodox religion, so much so that the topic became a Green hallmark. In the story "Archie and Angus," also found in this collection, Green chuckles over the new organ in the local church because, un-

The Land—More of an Enemy Than a Friend

like the parishioners, he knows the story behind it. When Preacher Sandy King—another powerful revivalist—inspired the parish to conduct a big money drive, the twins pledged fifty dollars for a new organ. A bad harvest embarrasses them until they trick the Widow Markham who has a standing bet of fifty dollars that she can outlast any man in bed. The identical twins take turns, exhaust the Widow, collect the fifty dollars, fulfill their pledge and, for their generosity to the church, are named deacons. Green savors particularly the way the twins convince themselves during intercourse that they're serving only for God. Green flirts with the same blasphemy in "Dr. Hyde," also from *Salvation,* when two drunks remove the plank that Hyde intends to use the next day for his miraculous walk on the water. The barb in these stories and plays is sharp, but it is not aimed at genuine religion so much as at the exploitation of poor folk by every new preacher who comes down the road. Green, who loves these people, shares their miseries, and refuses to have new ones pressed upon them in the name of God or of man.

This third theme, explored in so many different ways, emphasizes how deeply religion is rooted in man's nature. It does not inquire into the theology or psychology of the religious experience so much as it highlights the vulnerability of the peasant mind and the chicanery of religionists. The reader cannot conclude that Green despised genuine religion, that his mockery finally centered on God. In fact, as the next chapter reveals, in Green's most important writing, his plays and stories actually are God-centered. In them he works from the same material of the folk, but achieves the greater effect of tragedy: men, faced by the same bitter facts of life, rise above them, or identify themselves in the acceptance of the challenge.

CHAPTER 2

Rebels with a Cause

THOMAS WOLFE wrote as a Foreword to his play, *The Return of Buck Gavin:* "But the dramatic is not unusual. It is happening daily in our lives. We toil on a mountain farm to think bitterly on the unvaried monotonous grind of our existence. Here is material for drama in the true sense."[1] Everything that Paul Green has written on the folk shares Wolfe's views, for he centers always on *"the people* who live hard by the ways of nature and not by civilization and its sophisticated arts." He has rejected the usual relegation of such folk occupations to cotton-picking, milking of cows, and spitting across wide porches; for these ignore the fact that such great works as Sophocles's *Prometheus Bound,* Shakespeare's *King Lear,* and Ibsen's *Peer Gynt* deal with the folk as much as Erskine Caldwell does in his country novels. Folk drama is not an exclusively folk art in Green's judgment. The only distinction is that the subject matter is always the folk. Thus, Green found the farmer, or the tobacco grower, in his daily round of business in the fields and barns, a fit protagonist of tragic choice. The obvious pitfall that he or any author had to avoid was the submersion of his hero in the harsh environment. The proletarian novel, despite its originally noble purpose, attacks a problem or set of problems in such a way that the characters' individualities are buried. But, as Green's statement indicates, *"the people* who live hard by the ways of nature," always a man reacting to the forces on his life, was his interest.

I *The Field God*

Green wrote four major works on the white-folk material during this period before 1937: two plays, *The Field God* and *The House of Connelly,* and two long novels, *The Laughing*

Pioneer and *This Body the Earth*. Two one-act plays—*The Picnic* and *The Southern Cross*—complement them as minor studies of the folk hero. In each case, although less pronounced in *This Body the Earth*, the central figure is given a new start in life: through another person or new circumstances, a clear option for excellence is presented to him. Because of a weakness in his character, however, or a failure to understand the issue, or overwhelming external forces—or all three at the same time—he fails. His own set of flaws includes an impassioned temper, an abnormal tie to his parents and the past, deep fears of sexual inadequacy, overconcern for mores, or a combination of them all. Whatever the cause, like Conrad, Green dramatizes in these works a man in a moment of crisis who regrettably fails in his attempt to succeed.

The Field God, one of the earliest explorations in this area, opened at the Greenwich Village Theater, in April, 1927; ran for forty-five performances; and moved thereafter to the Cort Theater for an additional short run. At the time, Green had a certain reputation because of the Pulitzer Prize he had won in the previous year for the Negro tragedy, *In Abraham's Bosom*. The failure of the production of *The Field God* may be attributed, in part, to its inability to attract an audience interested in a man's quarrel with God and with his neighbors. The euphoric mood of the theatergoer at the time was unreceptive to a series of violent scenes which included the ravings of a grownup simpleton, ghosts, a suicide, the death of an infant, bizarre revival meetings in a parlor, and ragings against God: the 1920's had little time for any enemy of the people.

This obvious failure at the box office also suggests that the fault may have been in the script itself, or with the production. Indeed, the play still shows the effects of being written in four days; moreover, the topical life of the farmer limits its appeal for the urbanite.[2] But today's concern over God's death and its demands for authenticity in crisis-identity literature make this play's subject matter as current as anything on Broadway, a currency that suggests the need for a new production.

The play follows the plot line of Edith Wharton's *Ethan Frome*. The Gilchrists, a farmer and his wife, have achieved in their miserable marriage an accommodation that dissolves when her voluptuous young niece, Rhody, comes to keep house for them. She and the protagonist, Hardy Gilchrist, immediately discover a mutual interest that develops into love, one that renews life for each of them. But their relationship brings violence and death when the wife, Etta, suffers a stroke in the discovery, and dies after she invokes a curse upon them. Rhody and Gilchrist eventually marry, but the nagging community gossip and Rhody's sickness destroy the marriage. Thereafter, the neighbors literally bring Gilchrist to his knees in the church, "for converting to their God," until, as will be seen, he regains his former conviction and, with Rhody, strikes out on an independent life of his own. Unlike Wharton, Green was less interested in the circumstances of nature or fate which destroy the hero than the response that a man makes when under such pressure. As a result, Hardy exerts a major control over his own destiny, regardless of the threatening force of the community. Unable to overcome it with his free and loving gestures, and unable to capitulate, he would rather take his life than yield.

The first act presents Hardy's role as a maverick in the neighborhood. His refusal to be baptized scandalizes Etta, his Puritan wife, in front of the whole parish; he cannot accept the sacrament because he finds no distinction between Christians and pagans: "deep down people ain't Christian, Jew or Gentile, black or white, but just people." Nor will he believe that kissing, dancing, and other normal pleasures are sinful, no matter what scriptural phrases and arguments Etta and the minister use to refute him. But the greatest blasphemy lies in his assuming the role of Job, as he demands of God the rationale of violence and suffering. His heretical behavior casts a presentiment over the entire parish, and all the other participants in the tragedy, including Rhody, wait in fear for God to strike back. Like an ancient, guilty of hubris, Hardy prepares his own downfall.

The whole first act explicates in forceful language the rebel's opposition to orthodox Christianity. Aside from Etta's whining self-effacement over her barren condition as the cause of Hardy's unhappiness, this first section moves wth the same slow deliberation of the farmer's life; but, even with the minimal action, basic motivations and positions of the characters are established to determine future events. Life is hard, but God intended man to be so afflicted. Etta's Old Testament dependence on a

Rebels with a Cause

vengeful mysterious God—actually Green's third theme of religion but one used in this instance as a crutch—offers no rational explanation of the affliction; but it at least establishes a set of rules by which men live or endure. Hardy, who threatens the system with his disbelief and blasphemy, offers in its stead only a pipedream of happiness. But in this conflict of concepts, Hardy's humanism shines in the bleak, gray air; he anguishes over the suffering evident everywhere and over man's unfortunate duplicity through a lack of love. His own immediate solution takes him to the soil as a holy thing to be worshiped, but nature and an intrusive society make demands that prevent this fulfillment in the land. This combination produces tragic results as Hardy's goodness is thwarted at every turn.

Had Green completed his play, as he does at the end of the first act, with the death of Etta and her curse upon Hardy, he would have accomplished only another version of the *Ethan Frome* ending. But his purpose is to catch Gilchrist in the wake of the violence and death, to discover or to reveal what kind of man he is. Etta's death, which occurs early in the play, is, therefore, an incident that sets all of the other elements into motion. In the same way, Rhody has a function in the play for Gilchrist before she is actually a person herself: she symbolizes his sin of blaspheming God's law; she is the Jezebel, just as Etta says before she dies. Rhody is an object used by Hardy only as a psychological and physical relief to his anxieties.

In the first act, Hardy approaches life with the simplistic formula of the farmer who plots his days according to the chores to be completed, who continuously twits religion, and who lives with a verve that makes life tolerable or even blessed because of his love of the soil. But, in the second act, Green so complicates his character that the usual solutions will not do: Hardy is no longer merely the competent farmer, the lover of katydids and the blooms of the soil, or the independent carrier of the joyful news of creation to a sin-obsessed neighborhood. He is all of these, but, no matter how pure his intentions, he is also the cause of violence, hate, and death. In this development, the play moves into a new direction and away from the simple polemics against religion to a more vital area of human conflict and love and toward the reversal of tragedy.

The third act offers Hardy the real possibility of success.

Rhody's love and his crops which promise plentitude beyond his imagining suggest that perhaps a beneficent God does oversee human actions and hold in the offing for him a new life of joy. His paean to this God of abundance rings hollow, however, when his young helper, almost a son to him, kills himself because of jealousy for Rhody. The suicide not only strangles the resolution but signals a reversal of fortune. By the end of the year, Hardy and Rhody show decided signs of anxiety: she cannot nurse their puny baby; his sudden loss of a prize hog convinces him that his touch now produces death. Not even Rhody's continued love and her faith in his godlike strength can mitigate his self-doubts: he reads signs everywhere of his destructive influence, particularly of the long drought as another curse he has brought upon his neighbors. He agonizes over their suffering and over the wall between himself and these people whom he has loved all his life.

Compassion for them forces Hardy into a gesture that contradicts all of his past beliefs and actions: he submits to Brother Simkins and the praying congregation who will help him recover his "lost estate." But Hardy goes to the mercy seat as much out of anxiety over the things dying about him and Etta's curse as he does for love of his neighbors. Green thus plunges the hero deep into a rut of doubt and fear before the decision is made which determines his character: Hardy renounces the pietistic, superstitious rituals which bring God no closer and which provide no amelioration. Despite his love for the neighbors who have sustained him in the past, he again renounces their God and their religious ways as he regains his strength. In another form of religious ecstasy—one centered in Rhody's love and in a faith in nature—Hardy touches life on a higher level of joy. Witness to a divine epiphany, Rhody can only whisper, "You are my God."

Gilchrist travels full circle in his unintentional search for God. In the beginning, the life he extols springs from a smug satisfaction with his physical prowess and productive fields; from a truce that permits an endurable relationship with his wife; from a scorn for the sheep mentality of the Puritan folk; from an individualism untested by reversals. Only an abiding inexplicable love for his neighbors, which tolerates their religious quackery, keeps him from misanthropy. By the end of the play, he ascends to a kind of Whitman-apotheosis of man; but he does so only because he has successfully confronted the worst calamities life can hold. In his self-discovery, he transcends the daily, rutted existence that he had considered worthwhile but which had never been verified by experience in conflict. The structure of the play completes this theme: the action in the second and third acts literally tests Hardy's arguments in the first act against fundamentalism. Thus, despite all of his blasphemous denials of God's involvement in human affairs, when he and Rhody engage in promiscuous sex, God seems to wreak direct punishment in the deaths of Etta and Neil. When the two thereafter flaunt community ethics, God apparently kills their baby, the crops, and the cattle. The seeming connection of religion to these events persuades Hardy and Rhody to rejoin the Christian church: they know that God will be appeased only by such a conversion, that He will manifest His pleasure in the "great day a-coming."

But the wild gyrations and mad jubilation of the Christian witnesses to his conversion again turns Hardy away from the church before he recants in full. He rejects the orthodox formula which explains God's ways and His promises of a future life. What he only senses in the beginning he knows now as fact, as verified knowledge through his own strength and Rhody's love: God manifests Himself in a man's creative existence; He does not transcend human experience but is the sustaining force of daily life. Whoever appeals to the future for reward or punishment, or to any element beyond human experience, rejects the God who is life in humanity.

The play does offer one major difficulty in connection with Hardy's discovery of God in his own nature: what force or reason propels Gilchrist into the nightstorm to wrestle with God in the outdoors? And what epiphany does he experience that enables him to renew his naturalistic life of joy with Rhody? Green, who found philosophic and theological difficulty with this ending, aside from his dissatisfaction with it dramatically, completely changed the conclusion when he republished *The Field God* in the collection *Out of the South*. Rhody converts to Brother Simkin's Puritanism and leaves Hardy until he is ready to confess his sins: unable to capitulate or to survive as a solitary, Hardy commits suicide.

Both versions indicate how greatly Green hated the fixed attitudes and uncharitable ways of a society that was Christian in name only. In the first one, Green was more concerned with the character development of his heroes, Rhody and Hardy, than he was with an attack on the community. In the second version, Green forced Hardy into a suicide as a more bitter assault on fundamentalism, and on the moral order ascribed to a providential God. He defended this new ending in a rare, cynical statement, one that had less to do with dramatic necessity than with his own loss of patience:

> ...why should we always keep looking for indications of an inevitable and triumphant moral order and justice in tragedy? ...No, rather let him refuse to accept the final insult of bowing his will before a selfish and unjust God in whom he would not, could not believe. So his suicide is his one defense against hypocrisy, even his own.[3]

The suicide does justify Hardy to himself and leave the others, including Rhody, guilty of his death. Given the natures of Etta, Brother Simkins, Neil, Rhody, and the others, Hardy's prevailing, as in the first version, seems doubtful. Except for Rhody, whose promises of happiness prove to be illusory, everyone in the play constitutes only a constricted world of possibilities for Hardy, an outlook or a collection of eventualities sufficient to doom the hardiest of rebels. But his self-inflicted death also underscores Hardy's weakness when he fails in the test of solitude. Thus, no audience could respond sympathetically, regardless of the villainy of the antagonists. The nature of the plot, therefore, presented Green with a dramatic dilemma. His statement implies that an earlier philosophic bias coerced him into giving life to Hardy because he could not permit the "whited sepulchres" to triumph. The revised play attacks the enemy even more vigorously, but at the same time it risks a loss of the audience's empathy for the sake of dramatic logic. The play also discloses Green distanced twenty-six years from the artist as a young man who had wrenched the ending of the drama to fit a Romantic view of life. In both versions, nevertheless, like Job, the hero demands to know the reason for hate, violence, and suffering. The answers he receives are slightly different with each ending, although both evoke a tragic concept through the experiences of an uncommon man.

II   This Body the Earth

Hardy Gilchrist ends his isolation when he experiences a beatific love of the world, or he chooses to die in the face of overwhelming evil. Either way, he manages the situation; he remains his own man. Eight years later, Paul Green published the second of his two novels, *This Body the Earth*, in which the hero, Alvin Barnes, strikes the same pose, but does so in meaningless, crushing defeat. Green obviously intended tragic defeat for Alvin instead of ignominious death in anonymity. But the long novel leaves the reader only saddened by such ineffectual waste: he feels no exultation in the hero's death.

Through a combination of fierce desire and endless industry, Alvin cuts himself away from the white-trash members of his family, who "act like hawgs." He learns quickly that physical strength, dominant will, capacity for work, and shrewdness constitute power; and he sees how power shapes society and insures happiness. As a kitchen boy in the Byrd household, he is influenced by Dewar Blake, whose mysticism is balanced by a practical but religious love of the soil. Alvin learns from him that farming is a holy thing—to be loved, to be approached like the sacrament of holy orders. When Dewar's untimely death initiates Alvin to sorrow, the mystic's persuasive doctrine of the soil assuages the young man's grief. The teaching itself becomes a major thesis of the novel but one which has its antithesis in hard experience. The testing of beliefs in dynamic situations thus parallels the structure of *The Field God* but with totally different results.

Alvin throws himself into work with a zeal unmatched in Bethel County. Fearful of attachment to any other person or cause, he deliberately shifts about testing the different areas for profit. As a hand on the Clem Turner property, he rooms with the Chadbournes where he becomes devoted to the daughter, Ivy, but only as a brother. Although marriage does not fit in with his scheme for success, he rejects her probably more as a result of seeing his mother and father in their hate relationship. When he meets Ethel Layton, however, he falls in love and proposes almost at once, despite his expressed horror of marriage. She consents reluctantly, for she fears the slavery of farm life manifested in all the women around her. Part II of the novel, which ends at this high point of achievement, also shows Alvin in possession of the land that belonged to his grandfather. He will produce from it the richest cotton and tobacco in the country, "scientifically grown"; and the beautiful wife he owns will bear him outstanding sons. After drifting for so many years, he is now rooted in the ground and in society. All of Dewar Blake's words on the sacred relationship between the land and men come back, as a kind of ecstasy carries him into a love of all things.

The third and last part of the novel shatters this dream. First, Ethel refuses to bear a child, fearing that it will become another drudge of the soil. Then the tobacco crop is almost lost to the drought and the heavy rains. Struggling to save his investment, Alvin works himself into a complete physical breakdown. His recovery thereafter is pyrrhic, for his crops are virtually destroyed, his savings are lost through an embezzlement, and Ethel leaves him. Paroled after a jail term on a charge of assault on Ethel's lover, Alvin marries Ivy Chadbourne, who bears him four children; and they begin the cycle of tenant hardship and migration they had both known and hated since childhood. Alvin dies in a short time but only after he has exacted a promise from Ivy that he be buried without a headstone in the open fields to be ploughed and furrowed as part of the earth. The novel ends with Ivy's preparing once again to seek another tenancy where the living must surely be easier.

This Body the Earth moves consistently toward two contrasting points: the end of Part II, when Alvin has ascended to the top of the heap, thus achieving all his own promises of success; and the end of Part III, when his efforts and dreams sink in the hard, baked clay. The plot line, always clear, does not develop from Green's narrative so much as it carries forward in countless episodes the fixed purpose of the hero. Indeed, the unevenness of narration constitutes the most obvious and annoying flaw of the novel. All of Part I, for example, serves as a doubtful and therefore not too successful preliminary explanation for Part II, when the novel really gets under way with the appearance of Ethel. There are, however, some good portraits in the first part: Dewar Blake's reflections on life to a wide-eyed boy; and Alvin's trip to Fayetteville where he is initiated to sex through a prostitute. Notwithstanding these effective vignettes, had the novel begun with the courtship of Ethel—with Part II—nothing of serious consequence would have been lost. By deleting the discursive material of Part I—and a few episodes or essays in Part II—Green could have tightened the novel, thereby leaving the reader's mind uncluttered and cleared for some sympathetic identification. Chapters one and eight, for example, which tell of the blistering sun, of the grueling fruitless work, of the tenant migrations after every Christmas, convey the physical and spiritual aches of the farmer; but they only inform the reader and involve him intellectually. By contrast, Alvin's pain in the loss of his crops and Ivy's panic and loneliness as she takes her family on the road at the end contain the shared bitter experience of the whole of mankind.

Green's compassion for these sharecroppers appears on every page. As Robert Penn Warren has observed, a sociological idea pervades the book.[4] The injustice of the whole economy, the stupidities of the courts, the brutality of the penal system, the servile condition of the tenant who, in turn, unwittingly enslaves his wife, all chronicle the South. The lives of the humble ones who populate this novel—their homey conversation, the consolation from an old harmonica and homemade banjo, the promise in offspring, sentimental hymns to God and abuses of the preacher, cottonpicking, hoeing grass from tobacco furrows, nursing mules and killing shoats—are raised to poetry by an author who shares with these folk the endless struggle against the land. One reviewer, moved perhaps by his own farm memories, concluded: "If you cut this book, it will bleed."[5]

But *This Body the Earth* is not a blood novel of social protest, like Grace Lumpkin's *A Sign for Cain,* Clara Weatherwax's *Marching! Marching!,* or Upton Sinclair's *The Brass Check* and *The Jungle.* Green felt no less rage than these others did over the systems that dehumanize man; but, as an artist, he was more attracted to the consequences of the repression of the human spirit than to the discovery of the cause. In this novel, the centrality of Alvin's character enabled Green to avoid the heavy social tone and effect he might otherwise have set in the proletarian novel.

Alvin never moves away from the center of the story, so that, like Thomas Hardy's Jude, he takes on a stature beyond his nature and accomplishments. Full attention on him carries the very heavy implication that, if a man of his resolution, strength, and industry cannot make it, then who can? In this sense, Green insists upon the didactic, insofar as Alvin is the American Everyman. Alvin burns with ambition and rationalizes his twelve-hour-a-day job with the dream that envisions wealth, power, and prestige at the end of the road. For him, the drive fixes on the land as an end in itself and also as a means to complete the dream. Dewar's words, "Nature is God's great church," echo for him at every turn, although they conceal from him what is really a "Protestant ethic" which permits or even sponsors materialism.

On the night of his marriage, for example, Ethel and the soil are fused in his mind: both will receive the planting of his seed and reap a good harvest in a short period. This religion of the soil identifies him with Hardy Gilchrist, except that Alvin's holds no love-hate ambivalence for the farm. Even after his parole from prison, fifty-five pounds underweight, he still believes the earth will yield a reward for his puny efforts. He will not give up on holy nature, even to the last when he insists upon the planting of his body in the fields. This is not to say that nature's tyranny is an unconsidered possibility to him. At their first meeting, Ethel's father tells Alvin how he had once worked like a beast until he had felt himself becoming a dumb animal. One of the supposedly successful farmers, a "Yale graduate," informs Alvin that no one, with science or just dumb plodding, can conquer the stubborn earth. At every turn, Alvin sees signs of others who came to the soil with fresh hopes and new ideas, only to fail. But he is unswerving, like a priest returning to the sacramental land for sustenance.

To relieve this one-dimension fixation, Green adds a selfishness to Alvin's character that increases with his affluence and disappears in his failure. Alvin's first success, for example, culminates in the purchase of a new suit, which he guards from the rest of his family. Wearing it one day, he deliberates almost too long over its possible shrinking before he leaps into a pond to save his drowning father. This self-centeredness marks his relations with his mother and brothers, with Ivy later on, and with all people except those who can help him become "the best farmer in Bethel County." It drives Ethel away despite the deep affection she once held for him. Alvin's ambition flaws his character because he seeks only his own ends.

Even though Green intended this flaw to be fundamental in motivating Alvin's rise and fall, the novel as a pattern of tragic failure fails for two reasons. First, although Alvin's centrality holds the work together, the hero's external actions appear in clear, forceful images, and in dramatic, interesting narration;

but the reasons for his flawed actions can only be guessed at. The reader never comes to the inner dynamics that would evoke pity, fear, and terror over the hero's fall. Second, nature, fate, and circumstances do, in fact, overwhelm Alvin so that his nobility never appears on any cosmic level. Regrettably, he remains from beginning to end an anonymous, ineffectual farmer.

In *This Body the Earth,* Green continues his major theme of the land. He examines each new aspirant who approaches the soil, ready to compose it in his own image. The false promise of riches and life's ease quickly disappears in the reality of storm and drought, only to result in promises of sustenance with a new day. Green offers no explanation for the ambitious pursuit of the American dream, or rather, discovers none offered by his farmers. There is only acceptance of man and the soil as one, as the totality of God's great church.

CHAPTER *3*

The Tyranny of Family and Tradition

THE DEEP CONCERN for the common man that Green expressed in *The Field God* and in *This Body the Earth* clearly derived from his own life, although little could be gained here by a detailed cataloguing of the events of his life as analogues to the incidents in the play and the novel. But episodes of his youth, reported by Green himself in many places, and by Agatha Adams in her brief biography,[1] indicate the close parallel of Alvin's life with Green's. In addition, every word that Green wrote after 1927 echoes Hardy Gilchrist's basic humanism in the play. In fact, critics unfavorably impressed by both of these works suggested that the author's personal involvement in the material defeated any chance for artistic success: the emotional intensity of Hardy, for example, dissipates into Green's own transcendental frenzy, and the weariness of Alvin reflects Green's own loss of energy and hope. Although this view may in part be true, many aspects of the play and the novel are used so effectively as to obviate mere autobiographical reflection.

Green had no such problem of distancing when he wrote the four other pieces on the white farmer: *The Picnic* (1928), *The House of Connelly* (1928), *The Laughing Pioneer* (1932), *The Southern Cross* (1938). Subgenres, they demonstrate a stylistic range that balances the re-echoing themes. In them, the land again constitutes the total fact of life, always to be worked, but, ironically, always imposing its own form and value on the people. The land, or the caring of it, builds up in the character attitudes, defenses, weaknesses, and comformity to rituals which become a way of life. These pass down to successive generations, integrating tradition and mores, and, even more, inhibiting

The Tyranny of Family and Tradition

the will to new and different action and biasing the moral sense. This heritage of mixed or dubious values is what Green considers in these works; in them the land provides only the background, the threat, or the opportunity for him to examine his themes and characters. As a consequence, he seems personally removed and is thereby able to achieve greater effects.

I The Picnic

In the Valley and Other Carolina Plays, which appeared in 1928, was like two previous collections of one-act plays (1925, 1926) in that most of these plays examine the lives of the tenant farmers—white and black—in the daily round of existence. They do not raise issues beyond a man's conflict with the forces of nature and his simple pleasure in being alive. Cosmic problems, or any problems deeper than plowing furrows or curing children's pneumonia, are foreign to their interests and knowledge. One of the plays in this collection, *The Picnic,* is different: it studies dramatically a man's inadequacy in love as a consequence of bondage to his mother, to class distinction, and to the past. Only incidentally does the play involve nature or the land itself as a major factor.

In *The Picnic,* Ed Roberts, a wealthy landlord who moves in and out of many of these Bethel County stories, summons the courage to kiss Nancy Nelson, a tenant-farm girl, at the Sunday School picnic. When his act shakes him out of his abnormal shyness, he confesses his love and asks her to ride with him all over the countryside, regardless of what people will say. Nancy, who has already committed herself to him, sees him suddenly as a snob who has to work at loving her because of class consciousness. She also sees the problems growing out of his long celibate life with a domineering mother and his fears that all the girls in Bethel want him only for his money. She regards him now as a sissy, who says "Granny's alive" when he should let go with a good "God damn," and also as a coward who is wrapped up in his narrow self when life palpitates all around him. To prove her view of Ed, she shoves her body against his in mock seduction and lewdly challenges him to take her right there in the woods. The play ends when Ed, confused and afraid, runs away back home.

The short play suggests the goodness, strength, imagination, and vision that Nancy's love could bring to a man who lacks these qualities. Green presents a simple issue between a strong woman and a weak man; he shows us a man not decadent, not altogether impotent, but one whose environment cuts him away from genuine passions. His Puritan code and his sense of class distinctions affect his attitudes on sexual behavior, leading him to classify her as dangerous, even untouchable: "There's something wrong with her." Ed remains the rigid, neurotic man incapable of adapting himself to a new situation of love because of his inherent snobbery and a mother complex that holds him even after her death.

The Picnic broadened Green's view of the folk material and suggested the possibilities of choice and tragic failure that lay in the area of the Old and the New as social facts and psychological blocks; but the one-act form could not complete the discovery of love and subsequent incompatibility. Because half of the plot and play concerns the Sunday School teachers and the children's games at the picnic, little space is left for the swift action of the would-be lovers. The theme was resumed many times, but fortunately at a time when Green allowed greater room for exploring the emotions of the characters hemmed in by their peculiar brand of anxiety. His finest accomplishment on this theme, and perhaps of all his writing, was a full-length play written at about the same time, *The House of Connelly*.

II *The House of Connelly*

When Green wrote *The House of Connelly* in 1928 and showed it to his friend, Barrett Clark, Clark's impression was so strong that he sent it at once to the Theater Guild in New York. Purchased immediately by the Guild, the play lay at the bottom of some desk for three years until Eugene O'Neill's thousand dollars and other contributions enabled the Experimental Group, a junior partner of the Guild, to produce it in 1931 at the Martin Beck Theater. Green was somewhat disappointed in the ninety-one performances, but he was vexed by the three directors, Cheryl Crawford, Lee Strasberg, and Harold Clurman. He felt that their ignorance of the South, of farming, and of raw passions stylized the play and forced an ending not consistent with the logic of the action. Despite his displeasure, the play's critical success, on top of the favorable notices given *In Abraham's*

The Tyranny of Family and Tradition

Bosom in 1926 and *The Field God* in 1927, placed Green in critical estimate second only to O'Neill among the playwrights of the day.[2]

The House of Connelly centers, as the title suggests, on Will Connelly, the last of the male line, who administers feebly the broken-down estate long owned by the family. He is trapped by a mother and two sisters who expect of him behavior consonant with the Southern aristocratic tradition of living in gentle affluence, notwithstanding their impoverishment. His Uncle Bob —a lecher, drinker, and quoter of Latin phrases—reminds Will constantly of his own future image. Will fits into this wasteland, with no indication that he will change, until he meets and falls in love with Patsy Tate, the daughter of one of his tenants. Patsy deliberately seduces him: her desire for the land makes all other values only relative. But, when she comes to know him and suspects they both have something in common, her schemes are dissolved by love. Persuaded by Patsy's ideas of reclaiming the land, and, by implication, of recovering her own self-esteem, and drawn to her in the first stages of love, Will joins Patsy and Mr. Tate in plans for the restoration of the farm.

But the plans go awry when he is again seduced, this time by Essie, who, like Patsy, trades her body for Will's gifts. The ambitious program for the farm fades thereafter because of Will's debauches in brothels and his constant drinking. Patsy leaves him and goes to work in a town mill. Will, in self-pity, rails against his mother, sisters, and uncle as fakes and malicious corrupters of society—as pretenders to a dignity and nobility utterly lacking in the whole history of the family—and as the cause of his break with Patsy. This violent episode results in Uncle Bob's suicide, in his mother's lingering death, and in the flight of the two sisters to Richmond. Approximately a year after the girls' departure, Will fetches Patsy home from town where she has just become his wife. Swept up by the joy of a new life, he goes off against her wishes to bring home the two sisters to live with them, at which point two old Negro women, retainers in the family, smother Patsy to death as their wedding present.

Green writes elaborate directions at the beginning of the play. Decay must be emphasized in the staging, with fennel weeds that grow over the rotting fence and disused stile. Three stack poles in the field stand as a reminder of the gallows old General Connelly condemned his black son, Purvis, to be hanged on.

The rotting plantation and the curse of miscegenation lead immediately into characters who are less persons than part of the deterioration and signs of the Connellys' bedding with black women. The signs of the curse are two old women—Big Sis and Sue, fertile, sexual, mystically knowing—who dig at sassafras roots for tea, prophesy the dire events as a chorus, and ultimately act as Fate's executioners. Patsy, too, appears in this opening scene in the role she will play: she is appropriately digging berries, concerned over broken fences, but is fated by the Negresses' oracle to die in marriage. Will, white-skinned, lethargic, half-dead, fills out this first scene of revelation. His lack of virility is indicated by obvious sexual symbols: Big Sis cackles over the oft-repeated joke of Will's never shooting anything with his gun; when a flock of doves flies by, Patsy shoots and kills two of them with Will's gun when he can't fire; in all of their personal encounters, Patsy rushes in to fill the male role; the tenants echo Big Sis and underscore the gun scene with their complaint that there's no man in charge; and the old General might have been ungodly but he was at least at the center of things.

The first scene lays the ground work for the evolving theme expressed in the subtitle: *A Drama of the Old South and the New.* In Will and his four relatives, in the broken-down mansion—never lost throughout the play—and in the weedy pastures and orphaned Negro relatives, the South appears in its decadent illusions of past glory which cover up the realities of depravity, intolerance, and general decline of the human spirit. Before they can rejoin the human family, the Connellys must acknowledge who and what they are in a new and honest meeting with the world as it is. But, because they cannot, the family line is doomed. As a sure sign of their demise, the family gives a ball for a rich aristocratic outsider, Virginia Buchanan, who represents salvation for the Connelly family through marriage to Will. The same nostalgia for the past, this time when hope has gone altogether, appears toward the end of the play when the two Connelly sisters look over the treasured gold plates and the portraits of the Connellys: "It will always be this way to me, the way I've known it." If they could have faced the fact of miscegenation in the Connellys, if they could have manufactured enough love for the land to work in the fields, or if they had discovered that the only permanency in life is change, they might have been saved. But only Will recognizes the true Connelly lineage and confesses to the family breeding of Negro bastards and to the other injustices hidden behind frayed masks. Tragically, his acknowledgment comes too late for anyone to be saved.

Beyond this need for self-respect, one earned through introspection and admission of guilt, the play insists that the family must settle its debts with the land and the community. The time-honored acceptance of a class that, by its birthright, lives off the land like a leech brings its own consequences of demoralization as truly as any biblical law of compensation. Green never lets go of this theme throughout his writings: a man must work for his physical and spiritual sustenance and always close to nature. For this reason, his characters fill their lungs with lint when they work in the towns, or experience there the brutalities of sex, liquor, and mob violence. Nature scorches away man's investment of hope and energy; but, paradoxically, it alone holds a meaning for existence. The Connellys forfeited their right to the land when they moved from the cotton and tobacco fields into the parlors and perfumed bedrooms. Their degeneracy and the blight of the land are one.

They have an additional debt to the community, one tied intimately with the debt to the land. Through a sharing with new families, with commoners whose only right to property is their love of the soil, the Connellys can pay off their obligations to the hungry and the impoverished who have been victimized by them for over half a century. How simple this would be is suggested again in the first scene, in which the impression is made that the past without question marked an era of power, of a control that brought an order—even if unjust—to the society. General Connelly could bring down birds with his shotgun, and he could administer justice even when the punishment fell on his own black bastard son. But power has now passed into the hands of Southerners like Will, whose abnegation has produced disorder: the choking weeds, general indolence, and deep poverty. In this vacuum, the rising, ambitious poor folk, like the Tates, offer their minds and backs, spirit and love to reclaim the land and the family name. This love is what Patsy offers to Will, even if her motives are at first selfish, like those of the Connellys. The tragedy derives from the aristocrat's failure or incapacity to meet the commoner in genuine mutuality: specifically, in the doomed incompatibility of the two lovers.

If Green had pursued only these two themes—the debt of the

aristocrat to the land and to the common man—the play would have been merely another social protest of the 1930's. But technically, by centering the evils of the past in Will and the possibilities of the future in Patsy, and by developing the love conflict that brings the two together, Green executed a rare example of thesis and dramatic action intertwined. In this mismatched relationship, Patsy acts as the life force when she submits herself sexually continually throughout the play. Her first offering as a sex object suggests a devious character which fits her properly for entry into the Connelly family. But, paradoxically, it also shakes Will out of his death-in-life isolation, sufficiently enough that he takes inventory of his personality, thus completing the first necessary step toward reclamation.

The seduction scene was hardly intended to show the sordid side of Patsy, nor was it included merely to meet the obligatory sex episode for the Broadway theater. Too much depends on the scene for it to accomplish only sensational effects. The first act ends with this critical incident, and it poses a hopeful way out for the Connelly family: Patsy, devious or not, can reinvigorate Will. She is as gauche and common as the Connelly women think her; but she, and not the out-of-town aristocrat, constitutes the possibility of a new life for the Connellys; for her dark beauty, quick laughter, organization, independence, ambition, loyalty, and innocent sensuality can complement Will's strength and enable the whole family to overcome the shadow of the past. The loss of these qualities on Will underscores his tragic incapacity to make things right.

Two major psychological factors prevented a consummation for the lovers: one a serious blunder, the other a tradition-bound value too deep in the unconscious to be rooted out. The first ironically comes from Patsy's sincere intentions for the recovery of the estate. Her understanding of a man's sensibility lags behind her love at this point, unfortunately, because, in laying out the blueprints for the farm's reclamation, she inadvertently forces Will back into the little-boy role he played with a roaring father, a domineering mother, and nagging sisters. Her poor judgment in being the organizer again emphasizes for Will his inadequacy—even if he cannot verbalize it—and motivates a defensive self-pity which leaves him vulnerable to Essie's seduction. Will, of course, can justify his affair with the maid; for he merely follows in the Connelly tradition of bedding the Negro

The Tyranny of Family and Tradition

wenches. But he also knows that with Essie, with Patsy, and with all the members of his family, he is merely an object others use to acquire something else. Precisely because everyone makes clear to him that he cannot succeed on his own, he continues in this passive condition, and is actually sustained by the martyr image.

This tactical mistake by Patsy would have been meaningless with any other man. But the tragedy that results from it comes from the second factor, a much deeper cause: from Will's fixed values which are beyond his own understanding. Despite his own words to the contrary, caste beliefs, heavily fortified by a Puritan dual ethic, prevent him from really accepting Patsy as anything more than another Essie. Like Ed Roberts in *The Picnic*, Will cannot shake off this aristocratic prescription for the woman one marries, and the woman one has as a back-alley mistress. The demure, virginal Southern lady, a copy of his mother, lay in his unconscious, despite his protests to the contrary. Fornication with Patsy becomes her total self in his unconscious, regardless of her subsequent genuine acts of love. His inability to change with Patsy, coupled with the mishandling of his emergence from juvenility, wrecks his last chance for survival. Accordingly, Patsy's insistence, immediately before the catastrophe, emphasizes the lost promise of her love and his tragic ineptitude: "Right now we have to decide it, Will. Let them go. It's our life or theirs. It can't be both—they knew it. That's why they went away."

Green cast *The House of Connelly* into a frame of Realism, with the farming atmosphere and aristocratic decadence seen and felt in actions, words, and staging. He reached out for fuller effects through occasional Expressionist devices. The singing crowd of young boys and girls who comes to invite Will out at Christmas suggests visually the humanity in relationships dead all this time in the Connelly home. When Will's sister hits the gong, announcing the Christmas dinner, she produces a sound of the past in somber, melancholy tones that echo throughout the subsequent scenes. Uncle Bob's quotations in the dead Latin language similarly emphasize the Connelly's dated existence. The futile ball staged for Will's last hope in marriage expresses the over-all Connelly neurotic clutching at the remembered past. All of these symbolic instances, and others as well, contribute to the tragic effect.

Unfortunately, the final symbolic action stretches beyond the realistic probabilities and shatters the audience's empathy with its suddenness. Although Big Sis and Sue open the play and appear thereafter, they move outside the immediate central action and appear only as accidental, intrusive murderers at the end. The play works too consistently at the conflict, misunderstanding, and attempted conversion to be resolved in such illogic. It is clear, however, what Green intended in this macabre scene. Patsy's whole plan for success depended on persuading Will to kill the Connelly ghost: to remove from the scene, and from his sensibility, the last vestige of the past. His failure to do so, or even to understand, causes him, despite Patsy's warning, to race after his sisters at the end. In his failure to comprehend, or to shift from his old blood ties, he literally kills Patsy—as the last of the Connelly line, he kills her.

Green used the two black women bastard offspring of the Connelly men as the symbolic executioners, to illustrate all of the degenerative effects of slavery. The women are vulgar, superstitious, cynical, distrustful of the Connellys; but they are more incapable of change than the Connellys themselves. From their opening augury, they oppose Patsy's marriage to Will: they know no other way of acting than that of slave to master.[3] Patsy, who represents a threat to the old order, must be resisted. The signs in nature possibly are real to them: but, more likely, they use them as a justification for the girl's death. Whatever their motivation, they complete their service which leaves the Connellys intact: Will with his two white sisters and his two black aunts. They also demonstrate in the unexpected murder, but to a lesser degree, the twist of fortune that wrecks the future of a man: the tragic waste of a good person whose death can bring no new truth to Will as he goes back to his whiskey and whores.

Those who saw the production at the Martin Beck Theater left the performance with an entirely different impression: the play ended with Patsy as mistress of the plantation, as she brought to the isolation and loneliness of the Connellys a substitution of joy in family and community. She reclaimed Will through her buoyant love and attachment to the soil. But Green rejected this ending for the republication of the play in *Out of the South* (1939). The shift to a happy ending was forced upon him by the "yea-saying" group who manipulated art for social ends, by a coterie, he said, who saw in the play only a Socialist affirmation. The original ending of death became his final choice, one right out of life, in which Patsy is the symbol of the "creative process of life and the brave optimism of youth for a new day." But she is killed on her wedding night by the black executioners, "the goddesses of the Southern hearth, protectors of the old way of life and enemies to the new."

This ending does complete the bleak anticipation of the first scene, following it like an inevitable death ritual. But its supernatural or mythical substance shatters the tone that had been built up in the preceding scenes through the very real struggle between Patsy and Will. It is obvious that Will's hopeless inadequacy, representing decades of aristocratic depravity, leaves him unworthy of Patsy's offering, or of love on any level. In this regard, Green's thought runs straight to its mark. But the dramatic translation of the tragic punishment in the last scene leaves the audience with the feeling that something has happened beyond their understanding; that forces outside the events brought an illogical ending to an otherwise logical play. Perhaps the "yea-saying" group was really correct in its understanding of the meaning of love and reclamation in Green's drama.

The House of Connelly portrays the South accurately—too much so, according to Stark Young, himself a Southerner.[4] But Green uses a place he knows intimately only as a background for the larger issues already discussed. In this usage he no more falls into a provincial slough than Chekhov did when he centered *The Cherry Orchard* in the land he knew so well,[5] or when O'Neill set *Desire Under the Elms* on rocky New England soil. In these plays the characters act against a background to show their universal struggles; in Green's play the Connellys are used to indicate that the old must make way for the new, a cyclic process that brings fresh life in a democracy. But the old way contained its own beauties and strengths, its good and evil, that could have been resolved in the cooperative making of a new world. Uncle Bob obviously symbolizes this ambivalence. On the one hand, he tries to seduce Patsy, out of the tradition that the tenant farm girl is only another piece of property to be used; on the other, he tells Will that marrying Patsy is his only hope of recovery. Similarly, Bob commits suicide as a final act of despair after Will's tirade against the Connellys; but the suicide is also a last noble gesture to help Will. In this love-hate of the old, giving way inevitably to the new, Green shares with Chekhov a deep compassion for humanity in any place, at any time, as it passes through new-birth pains.[6]

III *The Southern Cross*

Green handled the same theme of the old versus the new years later in 1938 in a one-act play for radio, *The Southern Cross*. Another of the fine short plays, the intensity of action and decision produced a pathos obviously deeply felt by the author. In the basic problem posed and in its solution, the play is a smaller version of *The House of Connelly,* particularly as it centers on the character who knowingly holds the balance of his life in the major decision he must make. In *The Southern Cross,* Clara Olivier, bogged down on the decaying old plantation that was once a showplace of the South, rejects the offer of a new life that comes from Fred Jones, a commoner and another Confederate on his way to Texas. The conflict between them lacks the sharpness drawn in *The House of Connelly* possibly because Clara so obviously desires to get the Old South out of her system and to go off with Fred on an adventure to a new land. Convinced of all the reasons why she should go away with Fred, she still cannot leave. The "Southern Cross" has been burned into her. Although she is conscious of the stupidities of romanticizing heroes and events of a dead era, the Southern aristocratic tradition of bearing total responsibility has rooted itself too deep in her unconscious for her to free herself; she differs in this respect from Will Connelly only in her refusing to attempt an escape. The decrepitude of her father and the obligation of nursing him rob her of her youth, and she washes away the life force of the present. At twenty-five years of age, Clara memorializes her own death in the ritual of solemnizing the Confederate dead.

In this little play, Green shifted the emphasis from the rotting plantation to the Civil War, to the equally decayed mythos of the South that is supposed to insure a cultural integrity; but Clara's scorn of the war suffers from preachiness, probably because her words echo the author's deep feelings. Because of his disgust for the Southerner's romantic reverence of the Civil War, Green refused to give Clara the dignity that Chekhov gave to Lyubov in *The Cherry Orchard,* as she stumbles into the Russian future. Instead, Clara appears as a foolish lost young woman, waving a flag of the dead. Though yet alive, she will be buried in the old mansion, really another graveyard, a fit symbol of the dead Old South.

During this period of writing, Green seemed to be haunted by this conflict of the old and the new, disturbed particularly by his characters who discover the dichotomy and know the better values, but cannot regenerate themselves. This recognition and this diluted will have special application to Will's downfall. At the height of his attack on the whole Connelly line, Will finally comes to the basis of his self-pity, or of the guilt that renders him incapable of change: "All the old Connellys have doomed us to die. Our character's gone. We're paying for their sins." Like Clara, the dead past overwhelms him even when he can single it out as the foe. This same basic theme is developed by Green, one year after *The House of Connelly* in *The Laughing Pioneer* (1932).

IV *The Laughing Pioneer*

The issues in this novel, *The Laughing Pioneer*, are ultimately more precisely those of *The Southern Cross*. They are developed out of the inner dynamics of the characters, however, so that their emotions are seared for the reader in scenes as tight and dramatic as any Green ever wrote. The story is about another last person in the family line, Alice Long, daughter of Judge Long, one of the few genuine aristocrats Little Bethel County ever had. The Judge's illness and the need to care for him make Alice a spinster long before her time. Confused about her real motives, Alice kills her father when she has to fan him because of a bad asthma attack. Guilt over his death, gossip over her retaining the young Danny Lawton as a handyman in her house, and Danny's peculiar regard for her as a substitute mother prove too much for Alice; she slips into a fit and dies.

Despite the title and the opening paragraphs, *The Laughing Pioneer* is Alice's book. Placed in the identical situation of *The Southern Cross*, Alice commands herself and the situation by exerting a physical and spiritual strength impossible to Will Connelly, Clara Olivier, and Ed Roberts. She stands up to every reversal, ranging from a father's protracted sickness and death to a night attack by the Knights of the White Jessamine. Ironically, the one hazard she cannot overcome emerges in the possibility of a new, joyous life with Danny. Her ache for a man to fill her life, like the erotic dreams of the nameless spinster in "Her Birthday," seems relieved with his appearance. But he brings a greater pain, which she again sustains, in his failure to love her sexually as a woman. In itself, this lack could have been minimized by the intimacy the years would bring; but, tragically, her unguarded response to him motivates her matter-of-fact murder of her father, an act almost justified by the long years of frustration. She cannot free her conscience, however, as though in the act she killed off her whole heritage, an infamy for which she must pay with her own life. Thus, her last words in delirium before she dies sound her guilt: "The fan, the fan."

Green was on the brink of greatness with this first novel. The characters of Alice and the Judge remain long after the plot is forgotten. Alice, with her guilt working against her passions and her pride as a Long, emerges as a universal figure. Judge Long, although only a passing character, has a combination of lost dignity, compassion, and self-centeredness that suggests the bigger role he might have been given in the novel. Danny, next to Alice, deliberately lacks dimension; for, had he been given a greater spiritual strength, Alice would have successfully broken with the past and the tragedy would have been averted. From the very beginning, as a sick child, beaten by his father, he is a spiritual cripple unable to nourish a woman who requires a fuller sustenance. Green achieves a poignancy in this ironic mismatch of two searching lovers. The defeat at the end does not come from an outraged community, nor from overwhelming forces of nature, nor really from a guilt-ridden conscience: it comes from a man's insensitivity to the great gifts of an unusual woman.

The Laughing Pioneer falls short of excellence because the author kept his eye too long on Danny, even naming the book after him because of his unusual resiliency. The novel opens and closes on him; it gives him a far greater number of pages than any other character; it attempts an explanation of the joy nurtured in him by music and the soil. But he still remains unknown, a wispy character like the "no 'count boy." He never develops beyond his childish need for a mother's affection; his last words in the novel are little different from his first ones: "She was like my Ma—different, but like her. She'd look at me the way my Ma did. And she was good and sweet. . . ." His insensitivity to Alice's deep needs and to her extraordinary generosity would become a comic character but hardly one whose way of life implicitly suggests a correct posture in the face of tragic defeat. This juvenile sensibility, although it triggers the catastrophe, mars the over-all effect because it hardly makes credible Alice's break with the past.[7]

One other flaw rests in an unevenness of narrative structure: certain anecdotes receive an emphasis hardly consistent with their contribution to the theme. Conversely, certain events that cry out for full narration receive only a passing word. Most notable is the glossing over the raid of the Knights, when the preceding chapters had built a suspense for this event that demanded a full account. The greater unevenness arises from an already-mentioned previous difficulty—Green's excessive allocation of space to a minor character who never comes to life.

Despite these flaws, Green produced an effective novel. He presents a great illusion of reality in seemingly dull lives of farm people who are thrust out of their daily existence by events too great for their control, or for their understanding. In a combination of friendly satire and bitter social comment, of insight and lyric expression, and particularly of powerful character portrayal,[8] Green presents life as it is without excessive sentiment, or without pressing home any thesis. Although he does intrude occasionally to comment, he allows the bitter episodes to explain themselves in local expression but with an impact that ranges well beyond Little Bethel. Like the effects of a poem, the sombre mood achieved by *The Laughing Pioneer* lingers for a long time after the book is closed.

The subjects of these plays, novels, and short stories of the tenant farmers and their landlords were not chosen by Paul Green, the conscious artist. Green lacked the sophistication and range of the author who carefully selects one theme and subject over another. In them, he followed Koch's early suggestion that he tell in simple terms of something close at hand and that he remember how spontaneity must always precede form. It comes as no surprise, therefore, that many of Green's writings during this period are flawed by poor construction, provincial dialects, incorrect heightening of the tragic sense, and annoying didacticism. He avoided the study of rules, or of any formulas of art: "I haven't any dramatic technique. I merely tell the story, episode by episode. It seems to me absurd to try to force a story into a definite mould, demanding well-divided scenes, with a climax for each curtain and a cut and dried denouement."⁹ For Green, the real artist avoids deduction like the plague, for his proper subject is life, constituted of a million details to be observed.

By divorcing himself from the well-made play, all that Green had to do was remember the people he had worked with in the fields, laughed at over cornshucking, and hooted at in thumping revival meetings. Occasionally, he raised these folk to tragic stature, as in his two great plays, *The House of Connelly* and *The Field God*. Often, to reflect them accurately he borrowed from Rabelais a boisterous laughter that is expressed particularly in the collection of stories, *Salvation on a String*. Always, whether in tragedy or comedy, the struggle of man to survive, to maintain his dignity, to discover his identity, and to look for God is presented with interest, skill, and compassion. As one critic observed, in a review of *Out of the South*: Green has "the stature of greatness" because all of his writings come out of the heart of a man of long perceptions and great humanity.¹⁰ He loved his fellow men, no matter how common their nature and mean their accomplishment; his characters are all the Humble Ones, to be loved and helped. This openness to humanity included the Negroes who appear in abundance in his writings up to 1941.

CHAPTER *4*

Black or White—It's All the Same

WHEN GREEN RESPONDED to Koch's advice to write about what he knew, no matter how commonplace it seemed, it was natural that he included the tales and the lore of the Negroes he knew so well. Negroes, of course, had appeared in Southern literature before Green and Faulkner, but invariably as "darkies," as "nigras" who fill in part of the background for the white heroes and villains.[1] For Green, the Negroes were too vibrantly alive, too rich in humor and poetic sensitivity, and too personal in a relationship with God to permit them to fade into the corners of his plays and stories as maids and butlers, or as smelly cotton-pickers who know their place in Southern society. Green's interest was no assumed pose of a do-gooder; it sprang from the same source that evoked compassion for the white tenant farmers: a lifelong intimate friendship with Negroes—professionals and day-laborers—that began in youth.

When Green wrote of the Negro, he had, therefore, only to recall his own experiences and the stories he knew from memory; he had only to tell of the Negro as he knew him—as no better, no worse. But there could be no worse, no lower stratum in society; for "only the stones and beasts look up to the Negro." Crushed into invisibility, ignorant and deprived, the Negro had to look to his natural endowments for means of survival; he found them in deep-felt religion, unending resiliency, quick humor, and rhythm and song. They are not enough, Green indicates, particularly since the Negro is not aware of their unique qualities: the suffering and loss of personality have been too severe. Nevertheless, his trials "have taught him a dignity, a stoicism to evil and pain superior to that of his white neighbors. But his life is wasted in fortitude. He has little time for anything else."

However, even though Green suffered about the Negroes' impoverishment, raged over their being put in chain gangs, and complained of their "loose morals," he treated them as people who are only incidentally black, but who are Negro in the fullness of their culture. The authentic Negro atmosphere is there, and the peculiar Negro anguish emerges from economic and social enslavement. But the atmosphere and the fact of social deprivation are of no consequence when placed next to the discovery of these characters in their human context. Thus, the plays have a real dramatic life that derives from Green's uncanny sense for zeroing in on the moment of crisis, when the emotions, wishes, and memories of humanity—white and black—are at the brink of tears or laughter. Green was too much the artist to offer only social problems and solutions, or even problem plays designed to shock audiences into a social response. In fact, many of the tortured human situations presented disclose no villain, no enemy camp to be routed. Sorrow is just man's lot, and the Negro discovers that fact in the troubles his color has brought him; the white man realizes it in countless other but equally painful ways.

In 1920, Green wrote his first Negro piece, a one-act play, *White Dresses*. In 1941, he wrote his last, when he collaborated with Richard Wright in adapting *Native Son* for the stage. In between these works, he examined the Negro in fifteen one-act plays, twelve short stories, four dramas, and numerous essays.[2] In them, no Little Black Sambo scrapes and dances; no Stepin Fetchit bungles and mumbles; no big fat mammy smiles benignly over the whole human race. Men and women act out their tortured lives with the same ambitions and emotions, joys, duplicity and cooperation, sadness and defeat that mark humanity in any age and in any place. But, because they are Negroes in an America that defines their nature by the color of their skin, the emphasis in these plays and stories is on sadness and tragedy.

Like the white-folk literature, the Negro material falls into general themes, discerned now in retrospect but not so designed originally by the author. Also like the white tenant-farmer plays and stories, these themes appear as single or multiple, or as overlapping and complementary. They sum up the subculture as much as the imagination can create characters in human situations

Black or White—It's All the Same

without becoming sociological or philosophic treatises; for these themes remain subsidiary to the imagined persons who play them out. In addition, Green's works in no sense set the Negro apart, for all of humanity is so involved: only the expression or the emphasis remains peculiar to the one race.

These themes include six general categories. First, the suffering in the Negro's life provides the stimulus toward a redemptive love. Second, this same misfortune tests the moral integrity of everyone, particularly those who try to escape through compromise or the easy way. Ironically, escape means failure; for the compromisers invariably victimize themselves through an acute sense of guilt. Third, the suffering produces in a great many a cynicism that judges moral and cultural values worthless in comparison to the value of whiskey, sex, drugs, and other soporifics. Fourth, religion explain the Negro's continuance in deprivation, for he relies on a personal God who will ease his burden in the future. Fifth, as a substitute for religion, another way to escape from drab reality, the Negro, a born poet, casts himself through daydreams into an idyllic re-creation of self and situation. Sixth and last, the Negro exemplifies the virtues of hope and ideal democracy in his belief that an opportunity will be afforded him for a fresh start in life. All six themes, of course, rest on Green's observation, already noted, that the Negro's "life is wasted in fortitude. He has little time for anything else."

I *Redemptive Suffering*

This grim fact appeared with the greatest impact for the first time in *The Hot Iron*, a one-act play that could serve as a prologue to the theme, tone and effect in all the Negro material. In this play, Tilsey McNeill, a washerwoman and a farm hand, aches with migraine pains; with the burn from her iron; but, even more, with the fact of her three children under her feet, ill-fed and shabbily dressed. Her drifter-husband returns, obviously to bed with her and to take her few dollars. She knows he'll drop the seed of another child in her womb and then go back to his whores. When she refuses him, the husband grabs their son, thinking he's going for a gun to aid his mother. Tilsey cannot take any more, refuses to see her child beaten again, and so crushes her husband to death with the hot iron. She and the three children huddle around the body, awed by the violence, as Tilsey cries out, "We gotta have hep."

The fierce pain of human existence releases the cry for help in the last line of the play. Tilsey is, of course, a Negro; and the shirts she irons are for the white folk. But she is any human being overwhelmed by forces beyond her; therefore, the whites are not her enemy, and do not even have a name or a reference in the play. Nor does Will represent all that crushes her, although his dissoluteness causes the murder. He is only an outside force, no different from the headaches, the food shortage, or her burn. He represents to Tilsey everything that has struck her down—impoverishment, indignity, ravished sex, brutal labor—and everything that is sorrow. In one violent action she assaults life in the way it has treated her. She thereby releases the rage that she has been forced to contain; but, like any act of passion, hers avails her nothing except a momentary satisfaction. Her hopeless condition presumably will not be abetted by her employers; nor will the punitive law take into consideration any environmental provocation, nor the accumulated pain and abuse that led to her act of justice.

Green never wrote a more moving account of a person in affliction. Tilsey's succoring complaint to a deaf universe echoes Job's cries of despair and mingles in sound with Christ's own lament over His forsaken condition. At the same time, in a play as short and as unbelievably simple as this one, the woman takes on a heroic sensibility that resists the attitude of Naturalism: Tilsey refuses to sink under the extraordinary pressures of outside forces. When there is no food left in the house, she jollies with the children, sends them off to see if they can scrape up something, and tells them all will be well. When Will demands his sexual rights, food, and money, she resists him, despite the beating she is bound to receive. Her deep love for the children; her resiliency in the face of the dimmest of prospects; and her extraordinary endurance and capacity for pain inform the reader that man will never really succumb, so long as he can rally the feeblest "no" to whatever threatens his self.

There is no out for Tilsey, just as there seems to be no immediate solution to the afflictions of the Negro. But it is, paradoxically, when the downtrodden are pressed the hardest that their love assumes a redemptive character. In the short story,

"How Grandma Found Her Love," Grandma as a young girl witnesses the hanging of two white men and a Negro. The faint analogues to Calvary underscore the frightful moment when the three necks are stretched like those of chickens and the bodies swing gently in the pelting rain. She begins to faint when she is caught by a kind stranger who leads her away from the scene and into a long life of love, kindness, and marriage. Green seems to say here, without sentimentalizing, that even out of the most repulsive scenes of human degradation can come the goodness of love.

In "Frizzle," another story from *Salvation on a String*, the power of love again converts despair to exultation for the reader, if not for the characters themselves, when Mammy, the wife of a bullying Negro preacher, sacrifices the family's little dog to satisfy his demands. She and the children continue under the preacher's tyranny, but her forced act of love, brutal as it is for her and the children, brings them closer together. Tilsey, Grandma, and Mammy find no way out from the snarl and the viciousness that make up their lives. However, in a single gesture, or by a spontaneous act of generosity, each of them impresses upon this jungle existence the certitude of self in a relationship of fear, love, and sacrifice.

II Attempted Escape

Over the twenty-odd years he devoted to the Negro subjects, Green never departed from *The Hot Iron* concept of redemptive suffering. But he played on other aspects of it, particularly on the dramatic attempts of those who believe in some mistaken way that the American formula for success applies to them. It is human to pit one's resources against fate, or whatever it is that stands in the way of a man's rising to a more secure and peaceful life. The Negro, however, does so at the risk of losing even the miserable ease that he has gained by remaining invisible. His repeated attempts and consequent failures, even when his actions are not consciously motivated to improvement of status, constitute for Green the stuff of tragedy—and a second Negro theme.

One of these tragic figures is the pretty mulatto, Mary McLean, in the play, *White Dresses*. She has clearly been a frequent visitor to her employer's bedroom, but she informs her grandmother inferentially that Hugh Morgan is a good man, that he is deeply interested in her. Hugh's father comes on the scene and brings her a Christmas present, obviously from his son, but which he claims is from a Negro admirer. He says that Mary and the grandmother must leave their house if Mary does not marry the Negro who has been trying to court her for years. The present—a white dress—argues otherwise for Mary: just as any girl accepts an engagement ring, she takes it as Hugh's declaration of his love and intentions. But after the father leaves, Granny shocks Mary back into her "nigger reality" when she pulls out another white dress, one that Mary's mother had accepted in an identical situation. She then throws both dresses into the fire to "wipe out some o' the traces o' sin." The cycle of dreams frustrated is thus complete; both mother and daughter foolishly thought they were the lucky ones who could escape from the black constricted condition through sex. But the social and economic facts dissolve such dreams. No one escapes. Life can be endured only if one is a realist. Except for the slight interruption of Mr. Morgan and of the Negro suitor, Jim, this little play is little more than a dialogue between Mary and Granny which emphasizes social injustice. The play suffers from the obviousness of the successive generations—like father, like son—who bed with the pretty Negro wenches and who duplicate gifts at Christmastime. The condescending offer of a "white" dress to a black woman, no matter how light she is, is too therapeutic for the white man's conscience, and too patently a token for an audience to accept. The slovenly dialect of the grandmother too manifestly underscores Mary's white man's diction. And Granny's "I know something you don't know" makes her disclosure a climax and a conclusion that argue Green's theme of incest and miscegenation, but prevent the reader's feeling with Mary the full weight of her emotional discovery. The reader does not know Mary very well by the end of one act; he is only angered by the injustice of society.[3]

Green gives a deeper insight into another pretty Negro girl who sells herself in *The End of the Row*, another play in *Lonesome Road*. Lalie despises "nigger" features, diction, morals, and lack of ambition. She tells the three other women who are digging out crabgrass with her that she will move up and out of her depraved life. In the middle of her boasting, Ed Roberts, the plantation owner, comes on the scene. After a few stumbling openings, he proposes that she leave the fields to come to the house as a cook. She knows it is one step from the kitchen to the bedroom; that he will tell her of her beauty and his love; but that there will be no movement from the bedroom to the living room. Her deepest moral instincts force her to give back the twenty-five dollars he offers for her mother's medicine. He asks her to think about it and leaves the money on a bush. As Lalie returns to the fields with the bribe in her pocket, she, ironically, is crying over her rise in the world.

Her cry of anguish echoes Tilsey's call for help and mourns the compromise of self that the Negro is forced to make for bare survival. The Negro has no chance for economic and social betterment. In Lalie's case, because of her beauty and her destitution, her moral convictions have to yield when the alternatives are a mother without medicine and work in the blistering heat, or a life of prostitution. But it is this very opportunity for moral heroism, for shouting "no," that Green finds almost unique in the Negro experience. Lalie's tragedy results from her ironic capitulation to Roberts, after she had railed against the other women for carrying on with their "greasy Antmen." In acceding to Roberts, she commits a greater immorality than any of the other black women she scorns by perpetuating Negro servitude. Hers is a deliberate act, despite the seeming lack of choice given her; and, notwithstanding her own rationalization for the compromise, she knows what she has done, or is about to do, and cries over her moral deficiency.

Lalie is a hallmark for Green. In her he finds the anguish of all men—white or black—who discover in themselves the cause of guilt. In all of his works, he denies his dreamers the fulfillment in this life: the pursuit is an end in itself, one to sum up a man's virtue. But neither does he allow a man to heap his woes on a vengeful God or on a prejudice-ridden society. As for God, He in His mercy is indeed difficult to locate; and, as for prejudice, the Negro has merely to remove his shirt to show his scars. But Green, like the Greeks, insists that his characters discover the facts of their inheritance and environment and then ennoble themselves through a heroic stance. This intent takes *The End of the Row* beyond *White Dresses*. In Mary's case, the audience is presented with an ugly set of facts which forces the Negress into a black posture. In Lalie's case, Green converts the external frame into a more meaningful, conscious, emotional decision.

Thus, Roberts' bedroom will shatter Lalie in a way she would never experience in the backbreaking fields. There she could scream against the white enemy or against fate or merely against the hard facts of existence. In Roberts' arms, she will feel pressed on her the guilt of a self-imposed burden.

These "luckier" Negroes, ones with light-skin beauty, do catch the eye of the white man. Sex for these Negresses presents the possibility of escape, a way to drop the "nigger" role and assume that of the lover. But this method of escape only compounds the suffering. Moreover, the escape ends in Mr. Morgan's ultimatum to marry a Negro, or get off the property, or in a life of changing masters in prostitution. Green wrote the only kind of ending there can be to this kind of relationship in *The Goodbye*, a sequel to *The End of the Row*. In it, Roberts is saying good-by to Lalie as she leaves with their son for the North. She can no longer continue as they are, for Roberts is about to marry "respectably." She has made the mistake over the years of falling in love with him, and of thinking that he has responded in the same way. He complains instead that he has withstood the scandalmongers for seven years because of her and that now he is entitled to a family and a decent place in the community. He wishes he had the courage to confront his neighbors and tell them of his love for her, but it can not be done in the South. Even at this late moment, a flash of hope overcomes Lalie that he will do so, until he proposes again that she continue on as a back-alley wife. She recovers her determination, as she was not able to do in *The End of the Row*, and the play ends with her departure.

Here again, Green searches out the character's moral integrity instead of the situation. In one of the briefest plays of his career, he recounts by implication the bedroom action and the consequent child, the paternal denial, the child's bewilderment when told he must say good-by to the white man who is supposed to be his father, and the whole history of miscegenation that has woven into the South a fibre of moral decay.[4] But all of these elements are only background for the recognition by the two characters of responsibility for their own sufferings: Lalie's through the earlier acceptance of the twenty-five dollars and all that act entailed; Roberts' through an awareness of what love and heroism call for but his inability to defy community codes. This material was highly explosive in North Carolina in the 1920's. But the success of the play, then and now, depends less on the social issue of color than on the recognition of flaws by the characters. There is no suggestion that interracial marriage would provide the solution to a personal and community problem; instead, human beings appear in a moment of crisis, when they are given a chance to perfect themselves. If people have values that transcend selfish concerns, they can bring any problem to its proper solution—a solution that is not merely conformity to mores.

For the most part, then, Green subsumes the race problem under the greater consideration of how a man reacts to the pressures of his social condition—how he responds to attacks on his moral integrity. Thus, Mary and Lalie could have been moderately happy as mistresses to white men. They could have escaped sculleries and fields into properly arranged white bedrooms. Their mistake came in assuming that they could appease their own moral outrage in the bliss of love. Furthermore, they erred in thinking that the new role in the white man's world would expunge their inferiority. What they knew but ignored is that sleeping with Negro women somehow does not violate the gentleman's code in the South but that admitting them a position of equality would offend that code or tradition. In the one-act play, *Your Fiery Furnace,* a young boy sneers over his father's attempt to make his way up in the world: "He haint learnt adder all dese years dat de fust thing to be taught is foh niggers to keep dey place."

Like some piece of knowledge out of a race memory, the Negro knows what is expected of him in this tight social relationship, an expectation that has cosmic relevance. As one of the characters observes in another *Lonesome Road* play, *In Abraham's Bosom*: "Nigger's place down de bottom," for God intended the white man to be all head, the black man all heart. In such a split, the world has to be run by the white man or it will fall into chaos. In the same play, an oracular crone echoes this fundamental belief; white is white, and black is black, but white is best by nature. Judged in this light, Mary and Lalie, and many others like them, allow their moral values to be subverted by compromise to white demands. At the same time, like the Greek hubris, their reaching out beyond their station calls down the wrath of God, who is undoubtedly white. Through a combination of circumstances and wrong choice, Green works this second theme into tragic effects.

III *Easier Solutions*

Many of the characters in the plays and stories refuse to anguish over their lot. They ignore the abstract concerns of redemptive suffering and moral integrity and act out the third Negro theme of rejection or indifference. Keeping their place in a white-designed society poses the same difficulties for them, but they adjust to the reality of the imbalance with whatever is handy. Liquor, sex, dance and song, laughter,[5] food, superstition, and religion not only compensate for them but also manifest their weakness and strength, their memories and their hopes for the future, their sense of community and their alienation. One of them, Doug McCranie in the play, *Your Fiery Furnace*, insists that the Negro face the facts of his life, when he will not acknowledge his father's right to lead the black man out of bondage. The Negro must make his way in the world as it is and not as it ought to be. Doug says that the black man belongs to the pick and the shovel because the white man wants it so, that there never will be a way to change it. But, in the meantime, the white man cannot take away the Negro's good times.

Doug's independence influences old Muh Mak, who sees in his devilish attitude the only way in life for people like them. She would not change him at all, so long as he can bring to their low state a sporting time with the girls and music for them to dance. Both of them echo the old cliché that a white man would never stay white if just once he were "a nigger on a Settday night." Doug appears again as a "real sport" in *The Prayer Meeting*, one of the best plays in *Lonesome Road*. He and a self-proclaimed minister have a debauch in the making, with whiskey and two loose girls, when their grandmother breaks up the "Prayer Meeting" and throws both lechers out the door. In *In the Valley*, Bantam Wilson has the same values as Doug; when Bantam returns from the chain gang, all he wants is a bottle of whiskey and a woman.

These plays do not single out the black man as low and voracious in his appetites, but they do suggest that his license in liquor and sex results either from the white man's cruelty or from his imitating the white landlords. Green occasionally and inferentially asks how one can expect lily-white behavior when the one race has informed the other that the blackness has reached into his soul? When such a question is raised, however,

Green checks himself: his feelings run too deep in this area for him to mix freely his artistic aims with sociological explanations. In such instances, then, when he tells of Bantam, Doug, and others, he has no interest in cataloguing the vices of the Negro, nor in explaining the obvious causes of deprivation. He presents the full-blooded Negro only as he is: neither a villain nor a dreamy Uncle Tom sentimentalist. Green writes works of art which reveal "hidden corners of the soul and mind of the black man"[6] when he is in frantic flight or when he is at rest. Whiskey and sex are only part of the baggage he is forced to take in flight.

IV Religion and Superstition

But, if these panaceas enable the Negro to live in an illusionary state where he can camouflage the source of his indignation, religion constitutes for him the vital reason for existence. This religious experience is far more than a soporific, more than a way out of sorrow; it enables the Negro to discover a value in himself, one other than what the white man dictates: a deep spiritual sense that constitutes a dignity, an endurance, a conviction of future reward and immortality that are beyond the white man's understanding. This confidence rests entirely on the knowledge that "In God's bosom gwine be my pillah."

When Tilsey groans in pain over her ironing, she rallies her strength instinctively with a little song about God's mercy. Doug's song to Muh Mak and to his mother Goldie comes down to, "Judgment's a-coming. Judgment's a-coming"; and it moves Goldie to call out, from her own deep pain, "In dat great day, in dat great day, it'll all come right." The chain gang, at the end of *In the Valley*, continues in a similar religious ecstasy, one which blots out for them the horror of the body of their friend, lying dead on the ground. It also eases the weight of the pick and shovel in the boiling sun, as they sing out their hope in Jesus.

This fourth theme provides no theology of salvation, no rational argument of justice which would have Jesus punish the white sinners and open His arms to the Negroes. There is not even a half-quoting of scriptural passages to augur the vengeance of a wrathful Old Testament God, nor to evidence the love of Jesus for all men regardless of their color. Green presents only a kind of instinctive emotional definition of hope, one raised in song and dance to a fact of the present and a vision of the future. But, because it does spring from the imagination and finds immediate and simple expression, this religious impulse often turns into superstition. The minister himself helps to project this twist: because he somehow communicates with the spirit world, he speaks ex cathedra on all matters. The father and the other preachers, in the story, "Frizzle," are Olympian to Mammy and the two boys.

The dominating figure, in *Blue Thunder,* one of Green's rare Gothic plays, is a powerful black man who tells the three women with whom he has been living that he is the Great Popper, the Great King. He demonstrates his "conjurin'" power by forcing his cane to glide across the room to him and by commanding all the pots and pans into a wild dance around the women. In this fantasy, Green plays on the Negro susceptibility to the spirit world and to the acceptance of certain great men who commune with that world. The same awe, fear, and love are combined in the boarders of Quivienne Lockely's house in *In the Valley,* when John Henry enters the scene. Though he is dressed like a dandy and his manners are precious in the depressed setting, he carries with him an aura of magic when he admits that he might be the legendary steel-driving man. When he prophesies that Bad Eye will get new tires, that Farrow is headed for trouble with his girl, and that Bantam Wilson is off the chain gang and on his way home, Henry moves in mysterious ministerial ways that leave the others hushed and believing.

In this mystification that Henry weaves, one of the characters hints that he might be the devil: "somebody git him o' pair o' horns and a bag of fox-fire." The devil, "hants," and frightful curses to hell are always a possibility for Green's Negro characters. One of them, Blue Gum Ed, a murderer in the play, *Aunt Mahaly's Cabin,* in flight from a posse, hides in an old haunted cabin. While there, his own haunted conscience projects horrifying images: a glow under a huge pot which cooks a rat, a snake, a dead man's hand, and other witch's accouterments; a giant dog that drinks blood; a little faceless girl in a white dress; a Jack-muh-lantern, half-boy, half-dog. When he tries to escape from this nightmare, Aunt Mahaly herself appears, draws a circle around the guilty man for goblins to form their dance, and causes Blue Gum to drop dead. None of these haunts actually appear in the cabin, but Blue Gum's guilt creates images out of a cultural superstition that fuses moral behavior with the wildest products of the imagination.

The impact in this play comes from humorous treatment, even though the issue involves three dead men. The curse of an Aunt Mahaly—dead all these years—like the fulminations of Grandmuh Boling, and the damnation to hell of Blue Thunder after his regal boasting, is lifted out of the context of folklore and would seem to elicit laughter instead of wonder from sophisticated audiences seeing these plays. But Green's laughter is familiar: he does not reject these pseudo-religious stories, nor does he altogether believe them. He regards them as peculiar to the Negro culture, to be observed and believed or not. This intimate neutrality, or dramatized ambivalence, identifies the Green style in art—one that resists the homespun and the slick.

The subject in some cases depends too much on back-country experience and results in limited appeal. The play, *Supper for the Dead*, for example, is questionable in this respect. Fess Oxendine, a Croatan Negro, has assaulted and killed his daughter and has cut out his wife's eye. Queenie, an old crone intimate with the devil, appears with her twin daughters. Their beady eyes, long, gliding necks, and flicking tongues attest to the rattlesnake bite that Queenie had suffered just before their birth. Queenie chants out a command which brings back the drowned daughter to accuse Fess of his incest and murder. Moved by the incantation to a courage normally not hers, the half-blind wife shoots Fess, as the three witches slide off into the night.

When Green takes the audience into his confidence, as he does in *Aunt Mahaly's Cabin*, the conjured-up spirits, the curses of the sinners, and the over-all folk blend of religion, superstition, and inventive imagination are convincing. But, when he presents Queenie and her snake daughters to be fully experienced on the stage, he demands a set of beliefs which he otherwise ascribes as unique to the Negro, or to the back-country folk. What results is a field day for a director and an opportunity for the actors "to pull out all the stops" in presenting the magical: a corpse returning intact, a witch drawing threshhold lines, twins slithering about silently, a one-eyed woman killing her husband with the gun that would not fire before. To be credible, all of these incidents must be incorporated into some dramatic expression that reflects Fess's guilty psyche. As it is, the play says nothing beyond the portrayal of unbelievably grotesque action. It tells one again of the Negro's creative and fearsome involvement with the underworld as he attempts to discover Jesus in his soul. But beyond that, the play's Gothic trappings frame only a spooky story.[7]

The same cannot be said for *The Man Who Died at Twelve O'Clock*, one of the best of the one-act plays. In it, Green demonstrates the Negro's ability to laugh at his own peculiar mixing of the spirits, haunts, and the devil with his religion. Sally Evans, joyous over her impending marriage to Charlie McFarland, is destroyed by the news that January, her grandfather, while roaring drunk, announced that he was going to kill Charlie because he had informed the sheriff about his still. She and Charlie decide to play on a dream old January had: he would die on the day that the devil came for him at twelve o'clock. In a drunken stupor, January believes all the hell signs that Sally whispers to him. When Charlie appears as the devil, January shakes in fear. As the clock strikes twelve, he cries out that he will mend his ways. When the devil grants him a reprieve, he promises Sally and Charlie a complete reformation.

Handling material like this, Green is at his best. He has said repeatedly that he is not a stylist and that the whole school of playwrights trained by Koch cares less for the well-made play than they do for telling honestly some experience of their lives. But this play would have appealed to the Greeks as it does to modern audiences. January, the typical tyrant in his own household, is the Classical senex who deservedly falls before the young, sweet, but highly capable Sally. The haunting dream he carries around with him as a religious conviction and the roaring drunk he has been on combine to bring the action to a believable breaking point that is as much relief as it is comic. The pace of the play, too, prepares for this climax. It builds up slowly from the disappointing news to Sally, to the happy idea of the costume, to the whispered auguries of the devil, and finally to the face-to-face meeting with the devil. From this point on, the movement is swift and noisy until the end when January runs off to tell Luke Ligon about his experience with the devil. The dialogue complements this action, for it is simple and short: the characters say only what is necessary to move the plot to its hilarious conclusion.

There is no attempt in this play to lampoon the Negro. Sally and Charlie know instinctively that every man is persuaded by events that are outside the natural. They also know that Grandpa January is more vulnerable because of the visions resulting from alcohol. The situation fits in with the Negro's superstition but not in a unique fashion.[8] However, the events and the raucous humor do have the authentic touch of the Negro. When the Playmakers presented the play at Hampton Institute, in December, 1928, "fifteen hundred Negro students fairly rolled over on the floor in their enjoyment of the play." R. N. Dett, chairman of the Music Department, commented: "It was so faithfully and characteristically presented that Negroes themselves were pleased to the point of enthusiasm. I hardly find words sufficiently expressive to balance the accomplishment of these pioneer creators and interpreters."[9]

V Daydreams

The same charm of the Negro's imagination as a balanced approach, or a necessary adjustment to life, appears in Green's most successful one-act play, *The No 'Count Boy*. The dream to roam in foreign lands, to be a someone else for at least a little while, picks up every man waking or sleeping; but it has special meaning for the Negro and constitutes a fifth theme for Green. Lalie's dream to be the mistress of Ed Roberts' plantation, like Mary's wishful invention of Hugh Morgan's gift of the white dress, ends in the nightmare of reality. Blunted by the facts, these dreams are put aside for awhile; but they never disappear altogether. Without them, the Negro would have been destroyed in the very beginning when he was told he was a beast. As important in his life as religion and song, Green finds in the dream not only the Negro's defense mechanism but, even more significantly, the creative imagination of the poet. This interpretation applies particularly to *The No 'Count Boy*, a work which brings subject and form together in a way Green was never to improve on.

In this play, Pheelie is courted by Enos, a staid, reliable, devoted lover, but one as exciting as a plow in the field. He cannot understand her wild desires to go to places like Niagara Falls, or to wander like a hobo without a care for the chores to be done. Unexpectedly, a young boy appears in ragged overalls, playing a harmonica, "like it was a thirty-piece orchestra." In a few minutes he has won Pheelie to his way of life: he has come from nowhere, and he plans to earn his bed and board with his songs on the open road. His exotic talk only verbalizes Pheelie's earlier wishes to Enos: everything the boy offers is what she's been dreaming of for years. She'll go off with him that night, and in an old dress, with no provisions except what music can bring them. The bubble bursts when an old Negro mammy rushes in to punish the boy, her no account, lying son, who is now sniveling because of her threats of a beating. Pheelie is left with her empty dreams and Enos.

Green plays on the Aladdin theme of wishes coming true, but ones that do not come true in the here and now, where the sun comes up every morning and needs help from everyone if the day is to be completed. No one is really convinced, however, of this dull fact of life, least of all Pheelie. She dreams of far-away places; and, as though she had rubbed the lamp, the boy appears to take her there through music and laughter. The willed act to go with him shows she is more than a dreamer: she is a girl with strength, zest for adventure to fulfill a need beyond what the backwoods can offer; she is a person who can become bigger than Enos knows her to be. Despite the fact that Enos is himself a model of respectability, or that he offers a security and luxury exceeding the hopes of the average hired hand, there are desires in Pheelie he could never understand. This moment is the precise time for the boy to come into Pheelie's life and to expose the self that lies hidden deep inside her. Pheelie and the boy are one, and the Magic Land forbidden to grownups opens with his key so that she can put her picture books away.

Who could resist all these blandishments? No one, if it were true, or if one could come to the end of that road. But it is a "no 'count" desire that leads to ruin. If not, Green asks, why is the boy able to play only sad songs? The same boy who raves over the beautiful sights beyond the horizon sings no songs of joy. He is the one who warms himself in nature's bosom, yet he has just come from killing and eating a little bird. This Peter Pan and Pan ambivalence proves an irresistible lure for Pheelie, who is saved only by the boy's mother's appearance and her shattering disclosure of the facts.

The boy will obviously recover from his mother's beating: he still has his harmonica, and the "pitchture book" is an image in his memory. But, juxtaposed against Enos and his mother, he is shown up for what he is—a dreamer and a fake; he is promise without prospects of fulfillment. Pheelie's refusal to help him at the end and her bitterness with Enos indicate the difficult period ahead of her. But Green implies in the play that one should not take her problem too seriously. Enos' arm is around her even though she yells at him: "I don't want—I ain't ever gwine to speak to you ag'in! Oh, he's done gone. . . ." Since Enos' strong and warm love is flexible enough to allow for Pheelie's diversion with the boy, Pheelie's dashed dreams do not suggest a tragedy. Enos does offer a new house, fancy wallpaper, a good horse, babies, and the strength required to face each day's new problems. In a week or two, Pheelie will renew the quiet love she felt for Enos; she will probably even forget the sound of the boy's voice—will have no memory of the "only playboy of the western world" she came to know.

But how real, even though only for a moment, when the dream takes on flesh, Green seems to say; how different, at seventeen, when all the secret wishes are manifest in a person everyone knows out of experience. It is in this rare moment of anguish involved in growing up that Green captures Pheelie. No different from any other young girl, she is suspended between the world as she wishes it to be and the world as it is.

However, *The No 'Count Boy* is not merely a mood piece but a successful drama, one which brought Green his first commercial reputation, with the New York City Belasco Cup in 1925. All three characters are fully realized as distinct in their approach to the problem. The boy, of course, runs the risk of being typed a Puck, like Little Davy in *Tread the Green Grass* and Tommy, in *Shroud My Body Down*. But the Mammy's entrance, paradoxically, forces him into a cowardly reality that gives him dimension. Had he merely rhapsodized of far-away places, he would have been only a projection of Pheelie's hidden self. But with his mother's taking a stick to him, the reader knows that the boy has his own problems, for all of his dreamy talk. With the others, he is integral in a play of developed characters, tight action, and light fantasy.

In this little play, Green says that life simply cannot empty itself of the "no 'count boys." The dreamer dwells in every culture; probably a part of him lies secret in every man. But he is no ideal. The very charm of the play rests on the dream-reality, boy-Enos conflict that must be resolved if there is to be harmony in the individual and in society. Even in a play as muted as this one is in theme, Green impresses with the fact of life's ambiguities, with the mixed sadness and joy of existence.

VI A *Start in Life*

Just as the whites and blacks—like Pheelie, Mary, and Lalie—are no different in their attempt to forget the present reality through dreams, so the Negroes are no different in their desire to improve their economic condition through hard work and luck. When they fail—and their chances for success are so slim—Green finds again the stuff of tragedy. But the tragedy is that of any man who aspires and fails; it is not solely the downfall of a Negro victimized by a hostile society. That the Negro is and will be victimized Green does not dispute; but that his situation makes him different from an Antigone brought low by the civil law, or a Coriolanus scorned by his people, Green will not admit. This high regard for the Negro as a person indicates also the author's compassion for humanity.

In 1941, Green was asked to write a play for radio, as a part of "The Free Company Presents: A Collection of Plays about the Meaning of America." This year was one of stress, for a major war was about to begin at any moment. The writers who came together to spell out the vague American spirit, to see if they could put in dramatic form the cohesive ideal of freedom, included Burgess Meredith and nine other authors: William Saroyan, Marc Connelly, Robert Sherwood, James Boyd, Stephen Vincent Benét, Orson Welles, Archibald MacLeish, Maxwell Anderson, and Sherwood Anderson. Green stated at the time that this spirit could be spelled out in a conception of law which expressed "our idea of freedom and a good way of life . . . [which] guarantees the sanctity of the individual." When he presented his play as a development of this concept, it was appropriately on the sixth and last theme: the failure of the Negro to overcome his low state. Green entitled his deeply moving, one-act drama, *A Start in Life*.

A father and his son are awakened by Mammy on a momentous day which signals the father's start in life. Always a ditch-digger, like the other Negroes, he has saved his money to set himself up in business. He goes off with his son in the newly purchased but rickety old wagon to haul wood for a professor at the university. During the loading, the old mule, Mary, bolts, a wheel breaks, and the whole operation is halted. The professor, who pays him fifty cents for his trouble, orders him off the property as a nuisance. The boy is brokenhearted by his father's humiliation; but the father maintains poise until he arrives home. There, he beats the mule without mercy, threatens to beat the boy, and then breaks down completely in front of his wife.

In this final outburst, Green appears to be angry with society and with the professor as its representative villain. But this social comment is only incidental to the play. Far more important are the warmth of domestic love, the delicious odors of the breakfast Mammy makes for her men, the consoling silence she affords her husband at night; these detail the hope for yet another new start in life on the next day. The long morning ride to the client's house recalls moments every boy has had with his father sometime during his life. When the boy asks his father who is the best one who ever lived, the old man suggests that God must be, that the white man comes next, and then surely the professor. All this may be true, the boy responds; but he has his doubts for he knows his father is the best. The relationship of the three, despite the father's loss of temper; the feeling of the early-morning rising and the passage of time through travel and work; the homely details of daily life held up for admiration; and the stirring in human awareness of the possibilities that come from a start in life—all these make this play a work of art.[10]

This theme of a new start in life haunted Green. He worked on it twice again: in the short story, "Sun Go Down," in 1949, and in the one-act play, *Fine Wagon,* in 1959. In all versions, he translates the warm familial love that gives meaning to life. But he raises it to a level of "oughtness": every family ought to involve itself totally with each member, for a hurt to one leaves a scar on all. In turn, the larger family of society ought to take notice of every man. Even when the assailant argues correctly that he did not do anything, he remains guilty of ignoring his involvement in the other's downfall. But he ought to know, as a man, and even more as a sensitive, educated man, that his indifference or righteousness can destroy.

Green runs a risk of crass sentiment with such attempts to dramatize his belief in a mystical and practical democracy. His conviction that a man and society can and must bounce back after the worst of trials exposes him to cynical jibes of a vision of love and heroism that fails in daily life. But Green always looks at the worst that man and nature can work against a man. He particularly avoids solutions for his beleaguered Negroes; he insists, instead, that life has only the meaning that the responding man gives it; that the worst situation a man suffers can be met if he is assured of another start in life.

Pushed too hard, such a view ends in Rudyard Kipling's "If" or, even worse, in Edgar Guest's admonitions to live the good life. But Green, despite other dramatic flaws in some of these works, senses the sentimental pitfalls and therefore understates. This probably accounts for his ending *A Start in Life* with the father's tearful break, instead of first aid to Old Mary as a conclusion. The same thing is true of *The End of the Row* and *The Goodbye*. Economy of narrative through dialogue in these plays is not the only reason for so many things left unsaid. Green knew the perils of the prostitute theme, especially when a sympathetic response is called for; or the danger of a little boy on stage too long, wringing out the tears of the audience through his age and persecuted condition. Accordingly, he played down these emotion-fraught situations, so that they constituted only the facts of the case. The impact of the plays comes out of decisions reached from these facts, and out of the tragic results that develop.

CHAPTER 5

Three Black Lamentations: Abe, The Hymn, and Bigger Thomas

I *In Abraham's Bosom*

PAUL GREEN'S first modest national success came with the Belasco Cup award in 1925 for the *No 'Count Boy*. Although the Negro dramas were never produced by the Carolina Playmakers, with whom Green was so closely associated, he did enjoy a reputation in the regional theater by 1925 because of his plays on the white tenant farmers. In addition, his militant stance as editor of *The Reviewer* carried his name to other sections of the South. Even so, he was virtually unknown to the critics and general public outside the Carolina area when his first full drama, *In Abraham's Bosom*, was awarded the Pultizer Prize in 1927.

The play opened under the auspices of the Provincetown Players, at the Greenwich Village Theater, on December 30, 1926; but poor attendance forced an early closing. When it opened again, under the sponsorship of the Theater Guild, at the Garrick Theater, it ran for several weeks. A third production, again by the Provincetown Players, brought the total performance to approximately two hundred. For a playwright new on the New York scene, and with the built-in audience resistance to an all-Negro cast, this record clearly indicated success. But the critics did nothing to overcome audience apathy and enable the play to continue. Indeed, only Brooks Atkinson had no reservations about the play's greatness: "*'In Abraham's Bosom'* is the most penetrating, unswerving tragedy in town, and surely one of the most pungent folk dramas of the American stage." Despite its obvious dramatic flaws, the play demonstrated to Atkinson "a natural eloquence, a fervent sincerity and simple poetry, all pushing the fine action to tragic consequences."[1]

The other critics found in the play evidence of an important new author, but one who would have to school himself in the skills of the theater. Even Percy Hammond, one of the judges on the Pulitzer board who was lavish in his praise, considered the play too long, preachy, and even tiresome at times.[2] The over-all criticism ranged from Atkinson's approval, through George Goldsmith's enthusiasm for Green the poet of poignant, primitive emotions,[3] to John Mason Brown's complaint that "here should have been one of the notable plays of the season," but it turned out to be instead "a series of one-act plays without dramatic integrity, causing repetition and false climaxes."[4]

Green did, in fact, work previous material into this play of seven scenes. In 1922, he wrote the basic story of Abe's tragedy in the one-act *Sam Tucker*. In the following year, he refashioned the material in *Your Fiery Furnace*, in which Sam became the half-white, half-black Abe McCranie, tragically fated for destruction. The major shift emphasized Abe's son, Douglas, in such a way that the action unfortunately equally involves him and Abe. In 1924, the focus changed again, this time in another one-act play, also entitled *In Abraham's Bosom*. In it, Green successfully concentrated on the single incident of Colonel McCranie's beating Abe because he had struck the colonel's white son. All of the Negro's suffering explodes in the unjust punishment. The play ends in this felt violence, except for a lyric epilogue in which Abe's girl friend leads him into the woods.

When Green wove from these three short plays the Pulitzer-winning *In Abraham's Bosom*, he told the same basic story. Abe, the bastard of Colonel McCranie by a black woman in his employ, studies during the few hours he steals from work in the turpentine woods; at first, he studies merely to be literate; later, to be the educator of his people. Even more, he aims for freedom to be his own man and to be acknowledged by the Colonel as his lawful son. After Abe suffers a series of setbacks, the Colonel visits him and his wife Goldie, presents them with the "Howington Place" as a christening gift for their son, Douglas, and thereby tacitly acknowledges his paternal relationship. Abe's improved fortunes prompt him to open a school for Negroes and thereby fulfill the second part of his dream. The school fails quickly, partly because of the community indifference but mostly because of Abe's irascibility and severe discipline.

Fifteen years later, the family sinks to a new low: Abe shovels coal in a Durham power station; Goldie, an old woman before her time, launders clothes twelve hours a day; Douglas is a thief, spoiled by his grandmother, Muh Mak. Goldie persuades Abe to bring them back to the farm where Abe's white half-brother, Lonnie McCranie, who is now in control after his father's death, rents them a little shack. Again Abe's hopes rise and he attempts to revive his school. He prepares a position paper for the school board, but he is hooted and beaten out of the hall by the Klan. At this highly emotional moment, he meets Lonnie on his way home; in a need to lash out at anyone, he beats him to death and thus completes the action fore-shadowed in the first scene. Abe runs to his house, after he has seen a vision of his father and mother copulating in the bushes. Within the hour, the Klan circles his house to avenge Lonnie's death. Abe shrieks his defiance again, calls on God, and runs out to meet his executioners.

The play evolves through seven successive scenes. The logic of the action, however, seems to call for two separate acts: Act I, ending with Scene 3; Act II, including the last four scenes. Arranged in this way, the up-and-down rhythm, vital to the tragic end, is less obvious. Thus, Abe sinks down into the darkness of the woods at the end of Scene 1, after his intemperate beating of Lonnie brings on the whipping from the Colonel. At the end of Scene 2, the gift of the twenty-five acres restores Abe's faith, and his fortunes rise. The conclusion of Scene 3 again presents a broken Abe, defeated in his efforts as a teacher, brought low once again by his violent temper. At this point, Act I really ends, for the action begins again fifteen years after the school fiasco, with Abe's position even lower by the end of Scene 4, in the darkness of the city. With such a break between the acts, Scenes 2 and 5 could be seen as directly parallel: first, both occur three years after the previous action; second, Lonnie's granting Abe a minimal tenancy renews his confidence, just as Colonel McCranie's gift of the farm had given him a new start in life. The movement upward for Abe and his family again presents the chance for him to be the educator of his people, and his life appears to be a series of repeated opportunities. At this point, however, Green introduced the Klan antagonists as a major cause of Abe's reversal. If Abe had failed again because of his temper, as he had in the first act, the audience would have dismissed him as a psychological loser, an incompetent under pressure. The two scenes are analogous but only as one echoes the other, and only as both form a part of the up-and-down rhythm.

Scene 6 stands by itself; it is the dramatic fulfillment of all that has led up to it. Abe's violent temper—complemented by his single vision, and by his successive failures as an educator, provider, and parent—culminates in the terrifying murder of Lonnie in this scene. Abe, who heaps onto Lonnie's back the sum of his woes, stamps them out as he crushes his half-brother to death. His victim is, he knows, his half-brother—not merely any white man; and the act awakens from his unconscious the imagined or remembered copulation of his mother. Green, who is careful not to shock away the audience's sympathy, has Lonnie provoke Abe in two ways. First, he informs Abe that he has levied on his cotton crop and canceled their rental arrangement. Second, when Abe screams defiance, Lonnie crashes a lantern on Abe's head.

At this point, Abe is beyond reason; he is also deprived of hope in the future and of faith in his fellow man. Violence—the cause of his downfall repeatedly in the past—paradoxically, becomes for the moment a cleansing process. Before, "things" opposed him; but, in killing Lonnie deliberately, fate or whatever has brought him low is personalized so that vengeance is righteously his. Unfortunately, Abe is not purified by it: there are no values restored, no new insights gained. Instead of the serene ending he might have attached to Lonnie's death, or to any white man's death, guilt overwhelms him thereafter in the vision of his parents. He recognizes that, conceived in sin, the curse of God is upon him.

It is this haunting vision that Abe brings back home in the final scene of the play. When he learns that Douglas had informed on him to the Klan, he has almost no reaction, so filled is he with despair. But at this lowest point of his life, Abe again rallies his strength and casts himself into the hands of his God. God seems to respond, for Abe becomes the educator once again as he addresses the whole black race when he walks to confront the blasting shotguns.

In the most threatening situations, Green's heroes refuse to knuckle under, or to walk away from their chosen responsibility to a security in isolation. The enemy prevails, but the hero dies in one last attempt at engagement. This summarizes Green's approach to life, symbolized in the Abraham-Cain figure of exaltation and woe. In this play, neither white nor black, Abe is determined to live in both worlds. Properly named Abraham, the father of his nation, he attempts to lead his people into freedom, only to be mocked and rejected by them. His attempts to join his white father's world fail in the same way, although the great scene when the Colonel visits his new grandson actually produces Abe's conversion to a providential God. In this moment of rebirth, race for him disappears, and he lays his soul bare before the God of salvation.

Abe's new start in life is one he graciously shares with all those about him. But, because he fails to understand their reluctance to follow his lead he becomes a cruel deliverer. Goldie, Muh Mak, Douglas—all those he reaches out for—are destroyed by him because they fail to share his dream. Douglas, in particular, has his future unfortunately marked for him by Abe. Green writes a stage direction, suggesting that the effect must be one of Abraham offering his son Isaac in the ritual of sacrifice.

Instead of a leader of his people, like the patronymic Douglas, Abe's son becomes a tinhorn sport, a thief of anything he can get from life. His dedication to God by Abraham and his subsequent life of sin underscore his father's own history of failure. In addition, he is the connecting link of the play: Colonel McCranie rejects Abe because he is black, a mockery of the McCranie seed; correspondingly, Abe turns Douglas out of his house because he fails to fulfill the role Abe set for him at his baptism. In the same way that Abe struck back when rejected by his white parent, so Douglas literally destroys his father's dream to be the educator of his people. In another clear parallel, Abe cries out over his lost purpose and the failure of the others to understand; like an echo, Douglas protests over the same misunderstanding.

Abraham and Douglas, father and son, two would-be leaders, participate in God's design to take their people into the promised land. In their failure, Green suggests that the seemingly larger issue of race must not cover the deeper fact that salvation lies only within each man's grasp, literally in Abraham's bosom. Only Abe can save himself, and Abe can save only himself. But even with this inexorable law in operation, Green cannot allow the hero's charity, however misguided, to go unrewarded. Accordingly, Abe is not alone as he makes his solitary walk into the fusillade: he has cast himself successfully into Jesus' hands, delivered himself over to God.[5]

Abe is far more than the patriarch-in-failure of his race, the faint black counterpart to Abraham Lincoln. He is also Kierkegaard's Abraham, the "Single One" before God, whose "trembling existence" and acute suffering form the basis of his faith. Thus, Abe grows before God only as he is despised and persecuted; only as he realizes that before God, from the moment of his birth, he is a sinner. All his good intentions are worthless because of God's displeasure. But it is at this moment of despair that Abe leaps into God's hands, as he calls out a prayer of salvation. The responding voice to his petition, ironically, comes not from God but from the posse outside. Their final whispers echo Abe's lamentations in the same way that the hidden God listens to puny man's prayers.

In Abraham's Bosom is one of the great contributions to American drama. There are flaws, as the critics noted: it does repeat itself; the play leads up to the climactic speech before the school board and then covers the scene only with a flashback; at the same time, two redundant scenes are used to delineate Abe's poverty; and, at first glance, Abe appears to come full circle at the end, with death only a greater degree of reversal than the beating at the beginning. But the fierce power, rarely found in contemporary theater, the simple, beautiful poetry, the terrifying focus on race conditions in the South, all overwhelm these flaws. From the sequence of events, Abraham McCranie the Negro appears, authentically the man in his culture.[6] Yet, Abe falls before his dreams, only accidentally as a black man; he suffers all the tribulations of his race, but his tragedy arises from his own failings as a man. He fits into the pattern of the Classical tragic hero, for he is "Held down by limitations imposed upon him by his own nature and by his fellowmen, both black and white."[7] Few plays of recent times have stripped the tortured soul of a man so bare; few have shown the same exaltation of humble heroism. As one critic observed: "It has been given to Paul Green to show how the highest and the lowest can be implanted in a single human heart and from this tragic inner misery how the last drops of pitiful anguish can be wrung.[8]

II *Hymn to the Rising Sun*

In all of these plays and stories about the Negro, Green's deep anger, engendered by the enormity of social injustice, remained under control. The artist maintained a steady gaze on the properties of tragedy and comedy, and developed an optimism for humanity's future that refused to give way to outrage. Aside from this deep conviction that Green held of the artist's purpose and purview, the drama of social criticism itself made little impact between 1916 and 1929. Elmer Rice's *The Adding Machine* in 1923 and his *Street Scene* in 1929, John Howard Lawson's *Roger Bloomer* in 1923 and his *Processional* in 1925, and a few other plays before 1929 were the exceptions among the hundreds of productions throughout the 1920's. The times were not right for loud social protest, for the economy of the nation after the war had provided millions of Americans with an affluence they had not previously even imagined. This buoyancy prevailed in the large-city areas, particularly in the Northeast, in contrast to the South where a kind of plantation economy still obtained and where the black people's dollar income remained at the same low level for half a century. Green observed the economic, social, and spiritual depravity that resulted for the black man, and he fulminated against the abuse in lectures, essays, letters, and, by implication, in his plays and stories. But he was unwilling or unable to devote his art to social protest. His concentration on Abe's passion in no way skirted the evil of the white McCranies, but it indicated much more the depth of his understanding and compassion for the black man's tragic character. Concerning the white McCranies, Green continued to believe that the white man would develop a new and just ethical system in which the black man would not be given mere paternal handouts. In such progress to an equitable community, the white leaders would respond to their consciences and to the inevitable movement of the times. Accordingly, Green felt that there was no need for the artist to be the goad and the conscience of his age.

During the 1930's, however, Green changed his view. In this respect, he again shared the national attitude, or at least that of the artists during the depression. Playwrights and novelists then deliberately exposed problems as a means of awakening spectators and readers to social, economic, and political disparities in the nation.[9] Maxwell Anderson and Harold Hickerson raised the question of injustice in the Sacco-Vanzetti case; John Wexley proposed a solution for the Scottsboro trial in the play *And They Shall Not Die;* John Steinbeck catalogued all of the nation's social ills in *The Grapes of Wrath*: Erskine Caldwell cited the illiteracy, poverty, and physical malaise of the South in *Tobacco Road;* and James Farrell examined the alleys and backyards of South Side Chicago in his novels. The nation's mood had turned grim after the euphoria of the 1920's.

For Green and all the other aroused artists, inequities no longer could be dismissed by a principle of growth through laissez-faire; justice was no more to be equated with the majority will. Closer to Green's concerns in the South, Howard W. Odum and Harry E. Moore's *American Regionalism* (1938) and Gunnar Myrdal's two volumes on the race problem *An American Dilemma* (1944), forced upon America a new look at the Negro. Such sociological studies on race did not disclose new information for Green; they merely supplied a scientific basis for what had been implicit in his writings from the early 1920's.

Focused as Green's writing was by the social concern of the 1930's, his work took on a mood of anger. Two plays on the Negro were written in this mood: *Hymn to the Rising Sun,* a one-act play in 1936, and *Native Son,* a full-length drama written in collaboration with Richard Wright. *Hymn to the Rising Sun* dramatizes one brutal day in a Southern prison camp. In the play, there is no focus on either white or black race for, ironically, the chain gang was the one completely integrated institution in the South. The minimal action takes place at sunrise in a prison encampment. A youthful white inmate, Bright Boy, works himself into an empathic nausea over the cries and whimpers of Runt, a black prisoner who is serving out his eleventh day in a tiny black box as punishment for masturbation. The warden orders Bright Boy flogged for his demonstration of sympathy and then commands him to sing "America" in honor of the Fourth of July. The song ends as Runt is dragged out of the box, his body stiff in death. When the warden buries Runt, as he had requested, beneath the railroad tracks, he delivers a hypocritical eulogy on the spirit of Independence Day and American freedom. The play ends with the convicts marching off in lockstep, as an old man absent-mindedly sings "America."

In one swift and brutal action, Green presents a scene of depravity and violence, one almost unbearable for an audience to witness. The emotional intensity of Bright Boy's flogging and the appearance of Runt's body develop unexpectedly. The darkness at the opening of the play sets a mood of peace and security, only to give way slowly to the sunrise. The prisoners' awakening in the same way takes them out of their dreams into the stark reality of the prison, particularly after the entrance of the fascistic warden. When his sadistic, self-serving speeches are concluded, the violence erupts suddenly and then fades away just as fast into the final croakings of "America." The sharp contrast of rhythm and mood provides a shock of disbelief which turns into anger for the audience, and this reaction remains long after the curtain.

Green does not examine characters in this play, except for the warden and, possibly, Bright Boy, because he was intent on the development of a mood-thesis. The prisoners are muted ciphers; dehumanized, they are alive only as they devise means for daily survival. The strongest of them, Pearly Gates, endures as an obvious bootlicker of the guards, but in a manner not different from all of the others who have carefully studied the warden's moods for their own protection. Only Bright Boy fails to guard himself; as a newcomer to the camp, he still believes he is his brother's keeper. His innocence literally upsets the other prisoners, for his sobs at night disturb their rest. Such innocence and guilt deserve the whip, according to the logic of the situation; and for this reason Pearly Gates literally and symbolically holds the boy down during the whipping.

At first glance, the warden seems to be a deliberate caricature of the tyrant, just as the other guards are typical "rednecks." His sombrero, black leather bow tie, bullwhip and forty-five automatic fill out the convict-boss image. His clichés of speech are those of an illiterate who repeats commands as if he had invented them himself. His order-for-the-day speech on Independence Day reflects a chain-of-command mentality at work: how much of a father he is to them with his good discipline; how thankful they will be later, when they are tough and ready, educated properly for their independence in the outside world. His petulance over Runt's death—"Ain't that a hell of a note!"— underscores his total distance from the prisoners. But Green's is no mere portrayal of a black and white, evil and innocence, warden and Bright Boy dichotomy. Although the warden's cruelty triggers the violence, he appears on another level as a functionary for uncaring millions who use him as their instrument of justice, as a cover-up for their political and moral indifference: "Yes, sir, that's what they tell me to do to you, and I'm nothing but the instrument of the voters' will." For him, Runt's death and Bright Boy's flogging flowed from the will of the people—one manifested in a law and executed by the officers of the law.

But guilty as the corporate personality is, the play clearly indicates that the warden's duplicity breaks the chain of humanity. He and the guards corrupt the social order in their compliance, for each man must be his own moral censor. The warden properly indicts the professors, lawyers, ministers, and Rotarians who hide behind him; but, like them, he is not determined by the law. If he were to disavow the law, as he implies in his casuistry, all that he had to do was to walk away from the job. A man finally cannot slough off moral and social responsibility; and precisely this dilemma of obedience to the law and moral responsibility for the law adds dimension to the warden's outline and obviates a simple didactic effect.

"My Country 'Tis of Thee," sung by a beaten, nauseous boy in a prison camp on the Fourth of July, when followed by a twisted black body pulled from a sweat box, suggests melodrama at its worst. In addition, a play that contains little character shading in its emphasis on the opposition between good and evil is guaranteed to offend a sophisticated audience. But such is not the case with *Hymn to the Rising Sun*. The audience's shock in the face of violence and depravity; the fact of compassion in a situation where only survival rules; the boasting, self-serving monologues which echo a tortured conscience—all combine to integrate the action and theme for a final single effect. From its relevant title to the final ironic snippet from "America," the play moves on like a religious experience in which every part is vital to the final emotion. It is surely "one of the most terrifying studies of inhumanity ever written."[10] One does not wonder that Green still considers this play to be his favorite.

III Native Son

In the same mood of anger which provoked the writing of the *Hymn to the Rising Sun*, Green accepted an invitation from Richard Wright to write a stage version of *Native Son*. Although Green had the greatest admiration for Wright, the collaboration was not a success, at least not for Green. He attempted to make two major changes in the adaptation: first, to present the communism of the novel in comical fashion; second, to make the central figure, Bigger Thomas, "come to some sort of recognition that he too as a human being had participated in his own fate." Although Wright agreed and the first draft included these changes, he was ultimately dissuaded by Orson Welles, the director of the play: "I want the play to end . . . with Bigger Thomas behind the bars standing there with his arms reached out and up, his hands clinging to the bars—yes, yes, the crucified one, crucified by the Jim Crow world in which he lived."[11] At this late stage of planning, Green withdrew from the production; he was unwilling to compromise his concept of artistic truth.

Green's departure was hardly noticed during the publicity for the Mercury Production at the St. James Theater on March 24, 1941. The play received mixed reviews from the press, which changed to a generally negative reaction when the monthly reviews were published. The public, however, loved the bravura direction of Welles and the sensitive acting of Canada Lee, a pugilist turned actor. The play ran for one hundred and fourteen performances before it moved to the Majestic Theater in the following year for eighty-four performances. At different times since then, it has been on tour in all sections of the country except the South.

It is easy to see why the author of *In Abraham's Bosom* and *Hymn to the Rising Sun* joined forces with Wright. In Bigger, Green found a victim to be rescued and a set of crippling hindrances in the way to human dignity that demanded a public examination of conscience. The list of bigots who preyed upon the Negro in his previous works included only the Southerner. In *Native Son* he "saw a vivid treatment of the racial situation far beyond the Southern area . . . a psychological treatment of the corrosive effect of race prejudice."[12] He knew the inflammatory nature of the material would antagonize people in the North and in the South, but he believed that he and Wright would be able to translate the basic human truth of the novel and thereby benefit society.

This dramatic purpose characterizes Green's life and art. In no way, however, does it reflect the play that was written thereafter; for Bigger Thomas hardly typifies the American youth who is only incidentally black. Bigger is peculiarly a Negro; a victimized member of a minority group, he is turned into an animal, like the rat that invades his bedroom in the first scene. His reactions are completely visceral. Fear as an emotion proper to man, but one to be overcome, never enters into his consciousness. One of his friends says early in the play: "On his way now—Somebody gonna kill that fool yet"; another one agrees, "Or he's gonna kill somebody. Takes more'n a job to cure what ails him." Both speakers come to know and fear Bigger's violent animal responses even if they cannot quite verbalize them. The killing itself is instinctive when Bigger holds a pillow over Mary Dalton's face to prevent her calling out to her blind mother. Later in the play, he whips out a gun without thought to protect himself from sympathetic Jan Erlone. When he returns to the basement of his employer's house, his reaction to a newspaper reporter's leading question is to grab an ax. Intercourse with his girl friend, Clara, immediately after the murder, consoles him as therapy. But it is animal coition with a woman whom he later kicks in the stomach and uses as a shield against bullets.

This scene when Clara's limp body protects Bigger deliberately hints at Othello's despair over Desdemona's body. But Bigger lacks any capacity for heroic remorse: "All right, goddam it, I killed you. . . . Yeh, I said I would." Bigger's world had severed him from all relationships years before, leaving him incapable of love. In the novel, on the other hand, this self-existence rests on a documentary exploration of the sordid background and is complemented by lyrically beautiful introspection. As a result, Wright leaves the reader with a picture of a totally disintegrated personality.[13]

In contrast, the play, because of its objective nature, presents only the external difficulties of Bigger in a series of repelling incidents, all explicated by Edward Max, Bigger's all-knowing attorney. Bigger becomes something other than the lost black boy of Wright's novel, for his actions leave an audience shocked by the unwarranted violence and without any personal concern for his suffering and death. There are other difficulties as well, including one of form. Green took the three sections of the novel—Fear, Flight, and Fate—and staged them in ten sucessive scenes that were to be played without intermission. The structure holds for the first eight scenes, through Bigger's capture on the roof; but the two scenes thereafter—in the courtroom and in Bigger's cell—are unrelated to the previous brutal, sequential action. These two scenes comment on Bigger's crime; but, much more, they editorialize on life and justice, human nature, dignity, and normal aspirations. In these two appendant scenes, Bigger joins the human family when he emerges from his animal existence into a knowing, caring person. But they strain belief, for Bigger's potential for group involvement never appears before the conversion; no overt action anticipates this dramatic shift to his acceptance of society.

This change was obviously Green's addition to the play: Bigger must be afforded the chance of hope, the promise of the new start natural to every man. Early in the play, when Bigger receives the news of his new job, his mother says: "Maybe this is the real break. We are all so glad, Bigger, and we can quit living in one room like pigs." Bigger's new employer, Mrs. Dalton, echoes her anticipation, "This is your new start in life." Bigger himself, blown into sudden heroic stature by the murder he has committed and by the subsequent police hunt, considers for a passing moment a new beginning: "I'll be in them orange-groves soon . . . with the sun on my back." In a giddy state of illusion, he sees himself, when a plane flies overhead, as another Charles Lindbergh, but one with a different, more forceful kind of power: "An' when I light, ain't going to be no lot of people running to *me* with flowers. Hell, no! When I come, they run! Run like Hell!"

The start-in-life theme runs throughout Green's work as a trademark, as has been indicated already in the previous chapters. But, despite the obvious intention and the words spelled out here, *Native Son* is a "terrible drama that ends without tangible hope. It goes directly to first causes and it offers no ground of compromise."[14] Its awesome social preachment comes down to *"J'accuse."* But it is no tragedy, nor is it Paul Green. His fidelity to the novel—for all of its power and beauty—stultified the creative impulse he responded to in *In Abraham's Bosom* and resulted in two major flaws. First, and most important, Bigger never appears as a real person. Second, because Green concentrated on this attempt at delineation of the boy, he failed to be absorbed by the theme itself, as he had been in the *Hymn to the Rising Sun*. Nor would his original ending to the play, rejected by Welles and Wright, have improved the play. In it, Green contrives in the prison scene for Bigger to steal a guard's pistol and to threaten to kill both guards. Once again, he takes control of a situation, as he did when he determined the life and death of a white woman. At this high point of power, Bigger drops his gun; and, through a conscious act of the will, he walks into the death chamber, scornful of his executioners.[15] Such largesse in sparing the guards' lives, and a total understanding of justice and ethics are additives that do not flow from the action and character of the play, regardless of a shift in the final scene. *Native Son*, lacking character development and a universal theme, adds little to Green's stature as a dramatist.

Native Son, Hymn to the Rising Sun, In Abraham's Bosom, and all the other plays and stories about black folk that emphasized the sad lot of this minority group were not isolated protests from Green. His whole life and art are witness to his hatred of inequities, whether the victims are mixed-breed Negroes exploited by "pure-blooded" Caucasians, or unprotected American colonists victimized by European imperialists. Green has expressed equal fear of any individual or organization that takes up the cause of the offended and, thereafter, robs each man of his freedom in the very same way. Such an individual includes a Sam Adams who would convert an infant nation to his own ends, or a social organization that looks for cases like Runt, Bright Boy, and Bigger to use for its own progress. Green has consistently been the equalitarian, and he has insisted upon justice at every level for every man. Social theories do lie at the base of a government, but they have no value unless there is meticulous implementation and application of the laws. This pragmatic concern appeared in a letter Green sent to Theodore Dreiser on April 11, 1932. In it, he accused Dreiser and the National Committee for the Defense of Political Prisoners of sacrificing the Negro boys in Scottsboro. Green insisted that they were not "political prisoners" but prisoners of a local "attitude of ignorance, prejudice, hate and fear." Any outside interference, or new tangential argument, would only inflame the situation and ultimately destroy the boys. History indicates how correct Green was in his stance.

Paul Green's compassion for the black people reads, therefore, like an open book. Equally obvious is the sharp line he drew to separate the artist from the propagandist. When he allowed his rage to overcome his judgment about this distinction, the results were inferior, such as in *White Dresses* and *Native Son*. But, when he delineated his black folk as part of the human family who are incidentally black, he wrote works of great strength and beauty: *In Abraham's Bosom, A Start in Life,* and *The No 'Count Boy*. His lifelong commitment to demanding justice for all humanity, as a viable real possession to be examined and fought for continuously, not only informed his writing as an insistent theme but also, in its fashion, helped shape our contemporary attitudes. Long before any Northerners involved themselves in the unfashionable cause of universal equality which includes black people, Green worked in the unfriendly South to afford the Negro his rightful position of dignified freedom and unrestricted opportunity. In this respect, Abe always remains his spokesman: "We want our children and our grandchildren to march on toward full lives and noble characters. . . . God almighty knows they ain't no difference at the bottom. Color hadn't ought to count. It's the man, it's the man that lasts."

PART II

SYMPHONIC DRAMA

"Sing on, you young men and women, you sons and daughters of this land. And live, O Republic, in these thy children."

CHAPTER 6

Experiments in a New Form

PAUL GREEN'S writing smells of the soil and human sweat, and its sounds are the laughter and cries of his people. The sophisticated touch that marks the accomplished artist rarely appears in this folk literature which seems to disclose a Green who is the Negro hand or the white farmer immured in his tobacco fields. Never is there a hint of the urban traveler who spent a year overseas during World War I, a few years in Hollywood, two years on a tour of the European theater in 1928-29, and a year on a State Department trip to the Orient in 1952. Closer reading, however, uncovers what a profound effect the world travel had on the shaping of this literature, particularly the visits to Germany and England where Green came face to face with the kind of theater that had been unconsciously stirring deep inside him.

I *European Theater: A New Influence*

The European tour resulted from the obvious critical success of *In Abraham's Bosom* and *The Field God* which helped to win for Green a Guggenheim Fellowship to study European theater. The award proved to be timely, for the commercial failure of both plays dampened the high promise everyone had insisted was to be the playwright's future. The single-minded purpose of the New York theater—on and off Broadway—of emphasizing dollar return over integrity disenchanted Green early in his career. He was, therefore, not prepared to view the dramas abroad with any real enthusiasm until he discovered Berlin, Alexis Granowsky and Berthold Brecht. In a series of three letters to Koch, Green described what he saw and felt at the West End Yiddish Theater, where Granowsky was working out his innovations: a melange of material, "Grotesque and human, puppet-like, musicalized and stylized, unreal and other-worldly." He saw the plays achieving a marionette rhythm, like British pantomime, but with music and dance extending the meaning of the words that were always poetically there. He told of long discussions with Granowsky, in which the gifted Russian expressed amazement over the American uninterest in the rich possibilities of music drama, and particularly over the failure of the American artist to stage "the singing, the spiritual, the vivid religious ideology, folklore, the tall tales, the dramatic conditions surrounding the submerged yet marvelously gifted [Negro] people."

Green, who had mined Negro lore for almost ten years, knew even more than Granowsky the vitality of music in the black man's life. The musical pieces he had worked into his plays were however, only additives—little songs and ballads that filled out atmosphere, or that now and then uncovered a nuance of emotion. Prior to Granowsky's influence, nothing in his plays indicates the emphasis music would eventually play in his dramas. Nevertheless, in these 1928 letters to Koch there are hints of the direction Green was to take, including a specific reference to the Roanoke material that he was to fashion into *The Lost Colony*.

The antirealistic dramas that Brecht produced at the Berlin Opera also left a lasting impression on Green. Brecht believed that the Classical concept of the theater, which depends on casual relationships organically laid out in the plot, precludes any real audience involvement since all the creative work ends with the playwright. He felt that good theater teases the spectator by slant presentation, or puzzles him with only a hint of the story verbalized. At the same time, the whole story develops through dance, music, films, commentary, or any other device that jars the viewer into awareness, or that relates the events on the stage to the daily happenings of his life. Accordingly, Brecht used historic and current social matter without any pretense or make-believe to force the audience into participation with the actors. This audience involvement and Brecht's use of music—different altogether from the synthesis in Granowsky's productions—made an impact on Green that influenced the kind of drama he was to write for the greater part of his life. If the Guggenheim did nothing more than lift Green out of the doldrums in 1928, it served a good purpose; but it also provided an exposure that laid the groundwork for Green's "music dramas" that were to attract thousands of artists to North Carolina, Kentucky, Oregon, and other places remote from Broadway. The European influences paved the way for what was to become a total dedication for Green to a different kind of theater which he called "symphonic drama."[1]

Green never became a finished musician, despite the fact that his grandfather taught voice and that his mother—organist at the local church—considered Paul very talented. Even so, music occupied him all his life. His earliest memories include folk dances, folk songs, lullabyes, a fiddle, a banjo, a harmonica, some knocking bones, an organ, and a score of musical echoes that overwhelmed him when he began to write. All of them surfaced when Granowsky and Brecht pointed up the wider dimensions that folk literature could explore through dance, music, pantomime, and other imaginative devices.

Not that Green made a brand new start as a playwright. In reality, although the body of plays written after the 1929 tour properly comes under the different heading of symphonic drama, he never departed from Koch's original suggestion that he write only about things out of his own experience, and he never gave up writing about the folk. The essential difference between the writings before and after 1929 lies in the expansion of his vision, so that his later works contain the multitude of America, instead of the few folk of Bethel County. These later writings constitute more of an epic of the common people, even if, at times, their spokesmen come from the aristocracy. The people in these plays live hard by the soil, struggle against hardship, commune with their neighbors in joy and sorrow, and fill out their lives with the music peculiar to their situation. If before 1929 these folk were fleshed out in straightforward imitative drama, the people after 1929 are discovered as flesh-and-blood persons through the wider dimensions of music, dance, and spectacle.

A fusion of these different elements eluded Green for a long period. Thus, he wrote four "successful failures" in this experimental area before he arrived at a workable artistic form: *Tread the Green Grass* in 1929; *Roll Sweet Chariot* in 1934; *Shroud My Body Down* in 1935; and *Johnny Johnson* in 1936. Although they do not constitute Green at his best, these plays deserve attention as indicators of the success he was to have in symphonic drama after he recognized the reasons for the failure of these early attempts.

II Tread the Green Grass

When Green returned to Chapel Hill after his European trip, he renewed his friendship with Lamar Stringfield, a talented musician who had won a Pultizer Prize in music in 1928 for his suite, "From the Southern Mountains." Like Green, Stringfield had an intense interest in folk art; and he responded at once to Green's invitation to collaborate on *Tread the Green Grass*. The subtitle of the completed script indicates the emphasis in the play, and the area of Green's theatrical interest at the time: *A Folk Fantasy in Two Parts with Interludes, Music, Dumb-Show and Cinema*. The work ran into immediate trouble when the production at the Greenwich Village Theater was canceled only one week before opening night because of insoluble problems with the direction. The play had no New York performance, although it did open at the University of Iowa, in July, 1932, with a modest success, according to Barrett Clark's review.[2] The local audience there apparently agreed with Clark's judgment, but it is difficult to see how this work that Green himself called "a sick, wild thing" could then or now impress any audience—commercial or experimental.

The play concerns Tina Bassel, a young girl caught between the prohibitions of Puritanism and her awakening sensual desires that are stirred in her by a diabolic character named Little Davie. The orthodox argument of the play posed no problem for staging, for Green merely showed the preachers' tyrannizing of the cowed people in scenes taken directly out of his own experience. The inner dynamics of Tina resisted such direct expression, however, and account in part for the failure of the play. Green's solution to the problem is significant in the light of his later achievement, for he ultilized the technique of projection he had seen used at the Berlin Opera: dancing goblins and a Black Mass, fiendish manipulations of Little Davie, a community crucifixion of the local Preacher, and weird lights that flood the countryside. All of these are merely figments of Tina's fantasy and are projected on the stage through pantomime, dance, and music. But the projection did not succeed because the zigzag story line and Tina's roiling character, unrealized in any recognizable progression, left the audience only bewildered. The absence of any unifying or rhythmic harmony of the scattered parts prompted Green himself to observe recently to this author, "try as I might I was never able to drive any humanity into it."

Notwithstanding the theatrical problems inherent in *Tread the Green Grass,* the text discloses the same theme Green had explored successfully earlier in *The Field God.* The people are ridden by fears of sin, fears actually personified in the figure of Davie, traditionally the Devil in the Carolina mountain songs.[3] Davie was intended to be the cohesive agent of the play and also a shifting symbol of evil and good. As the symbol of evil, he is necessary to fundamentalist theology of sin in that he embodies the disorder and degradation the preachers fulminate against; he is the chaos that ensues when rules and prohibitions are ineffective. As a symbol of good, one far more difficult to comprehend, he is Pan who releases all people to the wonders of the world, to nature unshackled, but only to those who have eyes to see. Tina quickly converts to his vision when she recognizes in his goat mask the face of a saint. Her acceptance of a subversive figure, however, violates the community standard of morality. Like other rebels in literature, she faces either exile in license with Davie or conformity with her family and friends. Her capitulation to conformity signals Davie's loss of influence in an orthodox society, and a dull future ahead for a young girl with a lost dream.

Green offers in the play an insoluble problem, at least as it is posed for Tina. The conflict between the God that the churchmen proclaim and the God of beauty in man's soul and in the great outdoors leaves Tina in neither camp. But as opposed as Green is to the Puritan scorn of the body and of nature, he refuses to give Tina the license of nature alone: she cannot disparage reason and conscience which produce order in the community. A romantic ending would commit Tina to Little Davie's care, but Green rejects it. Instead, he has Davie leap off a cliff at the end as Tina returns to her stable but unimaginative husband. Green suggests that this future has to be, although her compromise points up "the distance that the sin-obsessed religionists of the South have to tread to a synthesis of body and spirit, to the day when mental health and unrepressed acceptance of life will seem like the sun—with the shining face of the irrepressible satyr."[4]

Tread the Green Grass does not exhibit Green at any high point of human appreciation. His pessimistic view hems in humanity with a Puritan fixation on sin and mocks any Christian church that has no room for a compassionate Christ. Thus, he introduces a minor plot with a young preacher who has faint analogues to Christ and who is rejected in the same way as the Messiah. Green presents the Preacher deliberately as little more than a shadow lurking in corners of the play, and he does so for obvious satirical reasons. But in this vague hint of a character, the playwright used a new approach he had admired in Europe: a reliance on Expressionistic technique, rather than on a full explication of character in causal relationships. In the same way, Tina never emerges as a recognizable person; she appears in faint outline, through song, incantation, dance, fantasy in pantomime, and garish impressions achieved through lighting and scenery. These prismatic glimpses of individual characters merge into denser views of large group movements, a density that Green believed added another dimension to the play.

This larger canvas of people anticipates the later dramas when the corporate personality dominates as though it were a human being experiencing personal joy and sorrow. But, however successful these later works might be, this first attempt to convey meaning through group experience ended in failure. The same vain attempt to bridge reality and abstraction occurred again in *Roll, Sweet Chariot*, another failure but one that seemed to fall just short of success. For those who know and appreciate Green's work, this play, with all of its weaknesses, holds a special place.

III *Roll, Sweet Chariot*

Green came to write this play over a long period. The original version appeared as the title one-act in the 1928 collection, *In the Valley;* it was expanded into a full drama, *Potter's Field,* in 1931; and then it was offered as a Broadway performance under the title, *Roll, Sweet Chariot*. It opened at the Cort Theater in the fall of 1934, and ran for only one week. As philosophic as Green was over the failure of *Tread the Green Grass*, he anguished over this play. To this day, he speaks of it with warmth and says, more in affection than with practical purpose, that he will one day revise it for production.

Green received no consolation from the critics at large, for they correctly predicted a quick closing even as they admired his imaginative reach into new areas of expression. Atkinson's comments were typical: "Instead of being fluid, a good part of the play was coagulated. In short, Mr. Green had not succeeded in sifting out the clichés of ordinary drama and creating, full panoplied, a new form."[5] W. P. Eaton, who had voted Green the Pulitzer in 1927, was even harsher; he considered the play to be "full of high-sounding language that only puzzles" and of songs and chants "which instead of making a symphony of the play make a Hampton concert. What dramatic story the play has bears no relation . . . to the conclusion."[6] Only Edith Isaacs, always a Green supporter in *Theater Arts*, commented favorably: "Although 'Roll, Sweet Chariot' failed at the box-office, the play and production are sure to be recalled in any history of important contributions to American theater."[7]

Miss Isaac's prediction was partly realized in time, for *Roll, Sweet Chariot*—despite its mystical aura, technical difficulties, and obvious incompleteness—indicated Green's gradual progression with music drama that finally led to *The Lost Colony* and to all of the symphonic dramas thereafter. The aim of this play was obviously beyond the artist's capabilities at the time. What he sought was the evocation of an emotional response from the most disparate of people—and he did so in the very same way that orchestrated music overwhelms and convinces.

Granowsky and Brecht's influence on Green is most evident in this play. The material came out of the Negro culture that Granowsky had inquired about. The scattered scenes which were carried on without intermission were Brechtean, particularly as they were reinforced by distorted lighting and by violent sounds, and as they dominated a deliberately thin plot. The story line concerns the inhabitants of Potter's Field who are haunted by the pressing fact of a new road that is to run right through their community. Their normally tense life breaks wide open when one of their worst citizens, Bantam Wilson, returns after a term on the chain gang. His violent quarrel with his wife's lover, Tom Sterling, results in his death and in Sterling's being remanded to the chain gang. Taunted by a white guard as he digs in the hot sun, Sterling strikes the guard and is immediately shot dead. The play ends in mass sympathy for Sterling, as all of the people of Potter's Field take up picks and dig the road that is to overcome them, as they sing out their hope for salvation in Jesus.

The site is literally a field owned prior to the Civil War by a wealthy man named Potter. Although the land may have filled out an impressive plantation at one time, during the time of the play it is a slum. As such, it symbolizes the wasteland foisted off on the black man, a potted field itself now threatened with extinction by the road. Potter's Field and the road that is the source of conflict command the audience's attention. Sterling at first seems to be the central character; but, even on the level of personal identification, he merges into the group. The road appears more central than any one person, for it remains as an awful fact that is just below the consciousness at all times.

The first scene demonstrates the kind of rhythm that the play will produce around the road. The seeming outward calm of Potter's Field, reinforced by the sounds of a guitar coming from a shack across the alley, is suddenly shattered by the scream of a whistle and the roar of an express train, sounds consonant with the periodic blasting of dynamite. The inner turmoil of all the inhabitants is exposed in one way or another, in a typical Green up-and-down movement, through song, pantomime, dance, and group movement; and it is projected against a background of crashing noise of the road construction. The dialogue, on its immediate level of communication, becomes poetically colloquial as it shifts into chant and then into carefully arranged music for solo voices, for instruments, and for chorus. The composition thus constitutes a symphonic play, for its effects flow not out of story, nor from a sequence of action, but from both of them combined with the central incident of the road construction that evokes emotion in music and dance.

The profound poetic element of *Roll, Sweet Chariot* demanded for proper expression a synthesis of the explosive sounds of the road-builders, the roaring of the wind, the dropping of the moon in conjunction with the tragic action of the characters, the voice of the law offstage, ordinary conversational dialogue, chanted conversation in counterpoint, dance movements in everyday situations, solo voices balancing a twenty-two voice chorus; and all were to blend with the forward progression of the play, in itself a seemingly insurmountable task. But the diffusion of centrality so that the people, and not any one character or set of characters, control the theme posed for Green and for the audience grave theatrical hazards. All of the individual problems and involvements of the people demand the audience's attention, and collectively they appear as a larger statement of the nature of man. But the line from the flesh-and-blood Negro reality over into the abstract Everyman closet drama is so thin that the playwright must be on his guard. Green does successfully write later a few plays in which the people, and the hero, receive his full attention. In *Roll, Sweet Chariot* emphasizing any one character to a greater degree might have unified the scattered parts into a total effect.

The embarrassingly short run suggests that the play did not achieve the purposed "dynamic finale." What was also demonstrated, however, was Green's resolution despite two failures with an art form; he remained fixed in his purpose to replace "the dry cacophonous wordiness" of the theater with rich poetic sounds. Despite a cycle in which "the curtain fell, the order came, the scenery was at the front door," he persisted in the exploration of "Strindberg's musical psychologues of the inner man." Aside from the natural balance he maintained through humor, Green took consolation, or resolved his doubts concerning this art form, in the words of a fellow playwright and friend, who had a similar failure in 1928: "I once heard Eugene O'Neill say, in reference to 'Lazarus Laughed,' that the theater would become a powerful force in American life only when some method was hit upon whereby the audience could participate in the performance somewhat as a congregation does in the ritual service of the church." Far more than O'Neill, Green was to work for this religious experience of the theater throughout the rest of his life.

IV *Shroud My Body Down*

A short time after the failure of *Roll, Sweet Chariot,* Green, working once again with Lamar Stringfield, completed *Shroud My Body Down,* an adaptation of *The Man on the House,* another one-act from the collection, *In the Valley.* All of the components of this work argued for success, with Samuel Selden, Koch's right-hand man and ultimate successor, directing the

Carolina Playmakers in the friendly atmosphere of Chapel Hill. The author exhorted the Playmakers to act out the play as if it were part of a dream: "To be produced with living actors as trained in the manner of marionettes and with masks when so specified." Unfortunately, the performance came over the footlights as straight Realism with only occasional Expressionistic effects, leaving the audience completely bewildered. At this time, it is questionable whether any different direction would enhance the meaning and dramatic effect of the play.

Green worked here once again with the difference between life as it is in its bleakness—expressed in the character of Oscar Graham—and life in the ideal—as it is lived in the wild desires of his daughter, Lora. The first scene, which handles a great amount of explication, anticipates in eerie overtones the dread happenings about to ensue. The second scene introduces Gothic trappings in the form of an Old Man who mysteriously becomes Lora's brother Fred, who possibly has been sexually involved with his sisters, who have since been drowned. The involvement becomes even more complex with the presence of a little Negro boy, like Davie of *Tread the Green Grass,* who is somehow connected with the underworld by his love of snakes and his sadism. Green, who knew that plotting of this sort results in the most vulgar of melodramas, therefore insisted on the use of masks and on movements like marionettes. In addition, he believed that, more than in the two previous experiments with this form, *Shroud My Body Down* would be carried by the music rather than by the characters and story. As such, it was not intended as entertainment but as "an experiment in mood and atmosphere . . . its effect upon the audience is meant to be more like that of music than words or ideas of fact."

All this intent makes good theory for the shaping of a form that could ultimately appear on the stage. Green said on one occasion that he knew the play was a failure; that his intention was sound even if the execution was lacking; that the setback made little difference because someone would eventually come along who could focus the play for full effects or use the form for better theatrical presentation. But in his admission of failure Green never suggested what probably was at the bottom of this worst play of his career: an inability to deal dramatically with the perverse side of human nature. Aside from the task of substantiating dreams on the stage (one he faced before and would face many times throughout his writings), neither of the central figures is motivated by the consciousness that Green consistently ascribes to human nature. Oscar seems only determined in his actions, from the fatal day that he renounces a beautiful and adventuresome girl to marry a sedate, dull woman. The situation is the same as in *The Field God,* except for the sequence of time and choice. Oscar and Hardy Gilchrist have much in common, although Oscar differs radically in his total incapacity for change, or for the discovery of joy in life. Hardy's bursting enthusiasm results in spontaneous cartwheels and handstands, but Oscar's measure of life comes down to the two meaningful realities of land and sin. His Calvinist fixation on evil has stultified his emotions and severed him from concern for his daughter. In turn, rejected in such a way, Lora lives only in her dreams, many of them incestuous transferences which fuse her father, brother, and Jesus.

Green certainly was not at home with the subject of depraved character. From his earliest writings to the present day, he has rejoiced over the buoyant, open-endedness of the human spirit. Early or late, he has been constitutionally unable to agree with the social scientists whenever they threaten the reality of a man's free will. Theological determinism, environmental behaviorism, or aberrant sexuality are foreign to his over-all view of man in the universe. No music by Stringfield and no direction by Selden could carry the inert weight of these characters, who were obviously dead to the playwright himself. Green implies how lifeless they are in his stage direction which calls for a central position for a grave on the set and for the quote of lamentation from Isaiah as an epitaph. Seen in this light, *Shroud My Body Down* is an apt title, perhaps the only good thing connected with the play.

V   *Johnny Johnson*

In November, 1936, the fourth and last of these "successful failures" appeared. However, in this case—*Johnny Johnson*—a fair number of critics over the years have consistently judged the work to be more a success than a failure. At the urging of Cheryl Crawford and the Group Theater, Green undertook the story, collaborating with Kurt Weill, who wrote the music. A recent Hitler-refugee, Weill renewed the friendship that he and

Green had struck up in Berlin in 1929 and accepted an invitation to work at Chapel Hill. This combination was complemented by the brilliant staging of Donald Oenslager, by the direction of Samuel Selden, and by the performance of an excellent cast that won unanimous "raves" from the critics. But, despite this talent, the play lasted for only a few weeks.[8]

The mood of *Johnny Johnson* seems to fit in with other war plays of the same period, such as Irwin Shaw's *Bury the Dead* and Maltz and Sklar's *Peace on Earth*, two savage plays which launched the Marxist group theaters into active social protest. There are echoes, too, from Pirandello's *Henry IV*, and seemingly specific allusions to Hans Chlumberg's *Miracle at Verdun*. In the Chlumberg play, a Conference of World Powers struggles for a solution to the problem posed by a group of resurrected soldiers whose cries for peace are disturbing the world. The whole theme of Green's play revolves around just such an irony. Hasek's *The Good Soldier Schweik*, and Stalling and Anderson's *What Price Glory?* were also well known by the author before he prepared to write his play. But the essential difference between Green's play and these other works lies in the effect produced through a blending of music, mass chanting, straight dialogue, inanimate objects that sing as a chorus, burlesque skits, and simple drama—an effect which leads to the triumph of the human spirit despite the great absurdity of war.

But *Johnny Johnson* is not an antiwar play, except incidentally as it includes war among the many causes of dehumanization. Johnny is an openhearted, if naive, tomb-carver in the South whose monument to peace is significantly never unveiled. He loves people to the degree that war cannot be considered by him as a solution to any problems. He refuses to fight in World War I until he learns that President Wilson regards the conflict as an end to tyranny and as a final step to world democracy. The play follows Johnny's career in the Army with a series of burlesque and serious scenes that mock the military mind and deride society's hypocritical demands for conformity and its craven position on war.

Johnny begins his quest for world peace in an induction center where all breathing men are accepted as fit for combat. He receives a bullet in the buttocks from his commanding officer as gratitude for his efforts at peace among the troops; he sprays laughing gas at the Allied High Command to prevent the killing of millions of men; and he finally lands in an asylum with a mental illness diagnosed as "peace monomania." A final scene, ten years after his Army severance, discloses him as a discharged patient who is selling toys to children in a last hopeless gesture of peace—as a Hitler-voice harangues the crowds in the background. In these wild scenes, where Johnny alone is the cohesive force, the author interweaves three distinct tones and moods: comedy, tragedy, and satire.

W. P. Eaton considered this mixture to be the precise reason for the failure of the play: the fusion of bitterness and tenderness blurred the aim of the play.[9] Green admitted later on that the story line and mixed tone were faulty and that they were held together only by Weill's incidental and sequential music. It appears now that Green did in fact so clutter the play that a kind of vaudeville diversion overcame the underlying cry for genuine compassion in human relationships. But this effect could not have been otherwise; for, just as Weill wrote a mockheroic overture as a comic clue to the ensuing events, Green joked with the names and characters of his people until they became caricatures. Johnny's sweetheart is Minny-Belle, as Southern in her speech and actions as pecan pie; but at the same time she functions as Minerva, with her paeans to the patriotic soldiers as they march off to war. Johnny's rival for her hand is Anguish, who is ineligible for service because of a self-inflicted physical condition. His millions earned from war munitions begin appropriately in the sale of mineral waters that are guaranteed to insure loose bowels. Johnny's commanding officer, Captain Valentine, fulfills the Hollywood image of the American soldier with his oily black hair, handsome profile, and heart of coal. The joking on names and persons continues with Major McBray, whose name indicates the quality of his psychiatric examination of Johnny. Johnny's name itself, because of unimaginative repetition, fits the anonymity of his role as a peacemaker.

If the names and typing of characters had merely underscored the profoundly moving events of the play, one would regard these devices as being in the rich tradition of serious comedy. But the diversions overwhelm the audience in scenes complete in themselves. Thus, the psychiatrists diagnose emulators of Saint Francis and Christ as mad, at the same time that they cannot remember their own names. The members of congress engage in endless and meaningless debate as the world careens to destruction. The military command reduces the fact of death in war to the movement of strategy pins on a map. Again, if such mockery had constituted the whole cloth of the play, the playwright might have struck a great blow against the stupidity of war. But, while generals and admirals are reduced to laughing idiots, Johnny must be seen as the Christ in an actual reverse pietà scene. The transitions are never made, and yet the movement is constant.

The general critical reaction understandably was an ambivalent one of praise and complaint for just these reasons: praise for a poet of such great intensity as the play expresses, but complaint because Green was not sufficiently the theater virtuoso to carry it off—if, indeed, anyone could make the play a success. The over-all result was bewilderment for the audiences who were used to theatrical structure and logic. And yet, the very things that puzzled everyone constituted some peculiar, undefined attraction. One reviewer observed that very few plays draw critics back for a second look, but that many of them returned to this one, discovered things they had missed the first time, and went away disapproving but unable to forget what they had seen.[10] Students who read the play today react with the same ambivalence: they are too sophisticated to accept the wild actions of a hayseed do-gooder, but they are unable to forget him.

Stark Young's observation after the opening of *Johnny Johnson* is applicable to contemporary student reaction. Young liked the production when his surest judgments informed him that he should not. He believed that the ideas were shallow and the movement bewildering, but that the performance unfolded an integral work of art that left one with a deep sense of sharing the hero's mission.[11] This participation was precisely the hidden thread that Green had been striving for in all of these music dramas, from *Tread the Green Grass* to *Johnny Johnson*. Here was the coming together of the various media that had always been available to the artist—a fusion of music, mass movement, and the spoken word—that could force the audience into a ritual participation. But *Johnny Johnson* does not wholly accomplish this effect; too much intrudes: Saint Francis of Assisi, Hitler's booming voice, Teddy Roosevelt and his big stick, Christ disguised as Johnny, dying soldiers in a field calling out to their mothers as an echo to the stirring sounds of the "Democracy March." In addition, the indoor theater boxes in the

Experiments in a New Form 91

imagination, leaving an audience unbelieving. Nevertheless, in this play Green and Weill brought to New York a new form that exploded the action into many exciting pieces, that demanded a different response from the audience. In the following year, Green moved the same kind of explosive material into the outdoors, when he produced the first successful symphonic drama in the country, *The Lost Colony*. With its production in 1937, Green's "successful failures" in music drama came to an end.

CHAPTER 7

Lost and Found — A New World Dream

I *History and Drama*

THE YEAR 1937 witnessed the coalescing of Paul Green's life and long-held beliefs. All great literature, he had argued before as a dramatist and philosopher, must work out to a positive act, or to the challenging statement of the hero, after he discovers there are no more turns left. Thus, Macbeth's descent into a final cul-de-sac produces the rallying cry, "Lay on Macduff!" Green's own Abraham absorbs the worst punishment that his own race or the white foe can inflict, and then goes out the door to his death, still singing out that the light will follow the darkness. Johnny Johnson—unjustly and erroneously adjudged insane and clapped away from the "normal" world for ten years and forgotten by the girl who once loved him—walks away into the dark whistling bravely. The value of humanity rests on such continuous affirmation of its own inherent dignity, or of its potential for greatness.

This vision of man, discovered by the ancient Greeks as the formula for *arete,* appears to be a simple fact of human existence to Green, one as natural as the drive for security, pleasure, and love. He suggests repeatedly, therefore, that man composes his own nature according to the manner of his response to suffering, pain, and evil. In these early years, long before the times allowed such statements—even in the North—Green prophesied that for this very reason the Negro must be feared in the future; for, ironically, the black man would forge the stuff of leadership out of the reversals of his life and would ultimately dominate the white man. All of Green's work contains one such scene of the low point of the hero before he determines his individualism and/or his destiny by the consequences of his reaction. In this respect, Green shares the twentieth-century existentialist belief that man is the maker of his soul.

The year 1937 also forced upon Green just such a decision. Up to this point, he had a solid reputation in the Tributary Theater, for his three collections of one-act plays in 1925, 1926, and 1928. He hinted also at potential greatness as a writer of fiction in his collection of short stories, *Salvation on a String* (1924); in a novel, *Laughing Pioneer* (1932); and in a second novel, *This Body the Earth* (1935). He had revealed himself as a writer of great, if uneven plays, including the Pulitzer, *In Abraham's Bosom* (1926), *The Field God* (1927), *The House of Connelly* (1931), and the brilliant one-act, *Hymn to the Rising Sun* (1936). The experience he had suffered in Hollywood from 1932 on left him with a self-image little different from the blurred one that emerged from his publications.

Even more, the extraordinary influence that Granowsky and Brecht brought upon Green, turning him toward a Wagnerian-type symphonic drama, had resulted in four plays that had consumed enormous energy and vaporized great hopes. The poor results of *Johnny Johnson* alone had cast Green's reputation to a low ebb, at which point he decided to return to the security of the classroom. The decision was more emotional than lasting, for in the next year he rallied his own powers and began what was virtually a new career for him. The early bitterness gave way to an acceptance of hardships as an opportunity to make one's own character. Any hangovers of the earlier mood were blown away in the subsequent paeans to humanity that were to constitute the symphonic dramas.

From 1937 on Green wrote and saw produced eleven of these dramas in ten different locations; one aborted play produced only as a pageant; and a translation of *Peer Gynt* that had almost all of the properties of the music drama. In these presentational epic dramas, the theme and characters are one; and the lofty theme is explored not philosophically in abstraction but through men and women in active, meaningful deeds dramatized on the stage. What all of them seek as a goal is constant in their lives, even when it operates in a limbo of consciousness: the completion of the democratic ideal as a way of life.

Although no one nation preempts this laudable endeavor, such a pursuit marks and unites America in the religious goal of fashioning an ever more perfect world for all men to share. As a uniting force, its subject matter and impulse come from all aspects of American life. In this appreciation of the nation as a proper subject for the artist Green draws together his long interest in folk literature and his newer intention to fuse it with music and dance as part of the American epic.

Already experienced in regional and commercial theater, Green knew the cynical reaction these productions would evoke from the professional theater people. Even so, he went ahead, convinced in his own mind that his symphonic dramas would "help establish worthwhile heroes." To fulfill his aim, he culled his epic figures from the pages of history but established them as ordinary men of the soil, full of ambitions, doubts, fears, love, and wonder. He presented them as the same shadowy figures his audience had been introduced to in school but in theatrical dimension that made them life-sized.

But Green did not simply move from the classroom at Chapel Hill to an amphitheater for a series of didactics. Just as Joseph Wood Krutch was strangely moved by *Johnny Johnson,* the audience reaction to these epic-dramas depends not on the author's explication of justice, freedom, or the democratic ideal, but on Expressionistic glimpses that demand involvement of the spectators. Stark Young's observation that the text read and the production seen are radically different experiences obtains to a greater degree throughout these plays. Contributing to this felt effect is the positioning of the theaters in the very spot that the dramatic action occurred in actual history,[1] so that the production literally is performed by the cast and audience as a kind of ritual in a "shrine drama."

Green's theatrical premise rests on two factors: first, his audience comes to the theater with a curiosity about, or a hunger for, history. Green could support his contention by pointing to the eighty million people who visit national shrines each year; to the existence of museums in any good-sized community; to the historical works that are best sellers every year, such as Kenneth Roberts' *Northwest Passage* and Margaret Mitchell's *Gone With the Wind;* or even to the growth in four years of the very expensive *American Heritage* from eighty thousand to three hundred thousand subscribers.[2] This deep interest in the

Lost and Found—A New World Dream

past leads to the second factor: mutuality comes from the historic discovery, a heuristic sharing, that produces a community sense of theater. Aside from the great number of tourists who come to these amphitheaters and experience for a short time this sense of community in the performance, the gathering together of the townspeople long before in the preparation and their continued involvement in the production revive the town meeting spirit of the early days of America. History brought alive on these huge stages awakens the viewer to his heritage of freedom, one won by men and women like himself in hardship and joy, and the experience sends him away conscious of his own obligation in the preservation of that inheritance.

One serious factor undercuts the theory and practice of these epic dramas, aside from the merits and flaws of each individual work. Green has produced eleven of these plays, and each one concerns momentous events as they occurred in the South. The one exception has Stephen Foster travel from Pennsylvania to Kentucky and back again, but even in this play the Southern atmosphere dominates the scene. Repeatedly, Green has argued for a mystical democracy that echos Whitman's in theory and desire for universal implementation, but he deals with his heroes only as they step out on the Southern scene. This practice is not accidental, for he believes that only the South could have been the location for Koch's ideas in the very beginning, and for the subsequent outdoor dramas. He sees the South as rich with dramatic material: folklore, superstition, song, hymns, ballads, spirituals, wild tales, feuds and prejudices, epical historical events and heroes involved in them. The basis for all dramatic literature has been the South's existence, he argues, particularly the tragic drama that comes from poverty, prejudice, and war. The South also differs from the other American sections in its idolatrous love of the past and in its communal sense of neighborhood, clan, and family. In addition, the climate of the South fosters an agrarian, outdoor people who are comfortable in the amphitheaters, which in turn heightens the outdoor effect of the historical material enacted on the stage.

The Southern renaissance of art supports much of what Green says here. But that the other sections of the country are barren of the cultural stimuli and effects vital to creativity argues out of existence the voluminous material written on the folk customs of the different regions. One wonders about the fact-fancy-myth of the Mathers, the Headless Horseman of Sleepy Hollow,

Johnny Appleseed roaming the countryside with his sack of appleseeds, or the exploits of the giant Bunyon in the Northwest. It comes as a surprise, too, that suffering has been mysteriously allotted to the Southerner alone when Green himself tells of the hardships endured by the great pioneers into the West.

All Southerners do not share this honorific view of the South's exclusive and effective use of historic material blended with tragic memory. In the 1966 meeting of the Modern Language Association, in New York, Professor Walter Sullivan of Vanderbilt University blew taps over a Southern literature that gazes forever inward. Much too arbitrarily but always with a single thesis in mind, he singled out only Flannery O'Connor as a Southern contribution to American literature, not because of her Southernness but because of her more universal Hawthorne-like approach to guilt-ridden man. In the same way, Allen Tate saw as early as 1925 that the South does not have an inherited culture like that of New England; and the Southerner is, therefore, unable to look at himself or his environment critically. The resultant escape from ideas encapsulates the region, forcing men like T. S. Eliot, Conrad Aiken, and John Gould Fletcher to leave it for intellectual stimulation elsewhere. Only if the gifted writer of the South looks outside can he free himself to ideas; for he then discovers what it is "to be a foreigner at home."[3]

Aside from the obvious limitations of regional attitudes in the full development of an art form, it should be noted that there have been successful outdoor productions in other areas where the community sense of theater prevailed: Lyn Rigg's *Toward the Western Sky*, in Cleveland, in 1951; Gladys Hoover's *Man's Reach*, in Pennsylvania, in 1956; Emmet Lavery's *Dawn's Early Light*, for the Oregon Centennial, in 1959; Kermit Hunter's *Forever this Land*, in Petersburg, Illinois, in 1951; and numerous others, including the surprisingly successful Martin Duberman's *In White America*, in New York City, in 1963. Of course, the greater number of the historic dramas have been produced in the South, but Green's view forces a wedge between the author and the American audience that need not be there, and it hardly encourages young playwrights from other regions to follow his lead. It can only be hoped that Green's recent musing concerning Massachusetts and California might lead into even more fertile fields. He believes that the Pilgrim adventures are ready-made for symphonic drama, as are the pioneering Spanish events, particularly in the establishment of Christian missions in California.

When Green wrote *The Lost Colony* in 1937, he did not envision any systematic examination which would program the whole span of American history. Nevertheless, his eleven symphonic dramas do fall into two distinct categories which cover a wide range of America's past. The first group includes four accounts of explorations to the New World by the English, Scots, and Spanish: *The Lost Colony* in 1937, *The Highland Call* in 1939, *The Founders* in 1957, and *Cross and Sword* in 1965. In each play the pioneers embark on a voyage to flee the prisons, feuds, and impoverishment in the old country; to better their station in life; or to plant their nation's flag on new soil. The struggle for survival in the virgin territory returns them greater values, or it destroys their dreams entirely.

A second group of epic dramas, less cohesively a development of a single subject, concerns an America only recently free from European exploitation and tyranny, and at the dramatic moment when she attempts to establish her identity. As such, she is seen forging a government of and by the people in *The Common Glory* in 1948 and in *Faith of Our Fathers* in 1951; then as weathering in 1861 her first and greatest crisis, in *Wilderness Road* in 1955, and in *The Confederacy* in 1958; as expanding into the West with new states, in *Texas* in 1966; and, finally as converting to Christianity the Indians in Ohio, in *Trumpet in the Land* in 1970. The discussion that follows emphasizes these two separate groups or subjects and deliberately wrenches the chronology of Green's writing. The logic of the subject matter seems to take precedence over any time sequence and still allows for comment on Green's artistic shifts and progress.

The form that Green used in the first of his music dramas—*The Lost Colony*—did not calcify so that every music play thereafter merely filled in the different topical facts but remained only an imitation. Green did vary his form to permit an emphasis on the people in the early dramas and then the more traditional stress on individual character. He also turned from the use of external elements of music, dance, and choral commentary to the integration of them as natural expressions and extensions of action. From rhetorical, declamatory speech, he changed to cadenced language and finally to flat dialogue. As in his fine essay about the nature and function of the teacher, Green demonstrated from his first writings in 1920 through the present time how much he was "Forever Growing."

II The Lost Colony

When Green was a student in Koch's class, he took a trip to the then-remote Roanoke Island, about three hundred miles away, just off the western side of Cape Hatteras. It occurred to him that the story of Sir Walter Raleigh's expedition to the area, which ended tragically in the mysterious disappearance of the last few survivors, might be good material for a one-act play. The resultant drama, written in 1921, presented a fictional study of Virginia Dare's life at Roanoke. Professor Koch, his colleagues, and Green all agreed from the very first that the play had no value.

Many years later, in April, 1936, Green was commissioned by the Roanoke Historical Association to prepare a pageant-drama to celebrate both the three hundred and fiftieth anniversary of the Colony at Roanoke and the birth of Virginia Dare, an event held sacred by the local residents. Because of memories of his original unworkable play and of an elaborate pageant-drama *Raleigh, the Shepherd of the Ocean*, written in 1918 by Koch to memorialize the tercentenary of Raleigh's death, Green accepted the commission; but he did so with mixed regret and anticipation. His regret arose from the succession of battles he fought from the very beginning with a public relations man who had circus effects in mind rather than religious ones. His anticipation rested on the promise that he would participate in the architectonics of the whole production as a consultant to Albert Bell, the designer of the theater, and as a selector, with Koch and Samuel Selden, of the cast and chorus.

As a disciplined artist after a period of sixteen years, Green resisted the impulse to reshape his original play and started instead on a long period of historic research. As a consequence, the two plays have nothing in common. The birth and baptism of Virginia are carried over from the early work, but they are only a small part of the vast sweep of events unfolded in the longer play. What Green brought from his early experience was more an awe for the enshrined area, one sanctified by the colony's actual presence there on Roanoke Island three hundred years before. The production was the first in Green's career that fulfilled all his hopes for the theater. It was performed in an arena seating twenty-eight hundred people, with three separate stages spanning one hundred and eighty degrees and with the sky as a roof. It included a cast of one hundred and twenty eight performers, comprising Federal Theater Project professionals, the Carolina Playmakers, and many other amateurs from the surrounding Roanoke area. The Westminster Choir came from New Jersey to sing the music composed and arranged by Lamar Stringfield. Samuel Selden agreed to direct the play, with "Proff" Koch as an adviser.

Green's idea of a theater was further realized when the financing and costuming of the production were arranged through the local folk, with a generous assist from the Works Project Administration. The final satisfying touch came in the admission charge of one dollar to the Waterside Theater to people who came in shirtsleeves. This was the people's theater Green had talked and written about for years, one that opened apppropriately on July 4, 1937. Except for the war years—1942-46—it has run every night during the summer season, increasing in attendance each year. In 1966 alone, over one hundred and forty-five thousand people paid admission to see the play. Its first year was distinguished by the attendance of President Roosevelt, who spoke glowingly of the rare accomplishments in this outpost of the country. Thereafter, it was virtually cast into perpetuity by an Act of Congress that named Fort Raleigh a national shrine and by an appropriation of a yearly stipend of ten thousand dollars by the North Carolina Legislature. *The Lost Colony*, begun as a celebration of a brave people lost in a hopeless adventure, is now itself an integral part of the American Way and also a vital contribution to the mythos of the country.

The Lost Colony tells of the dream of Sir Walter Raleigh to extend English dominion to the New World. His vision comes to reality in July, 1584, when Philip Amadas and Arthur Barlowe land with their crew in "the goodliest land under the cope of heaven"—a land like the island in the Ocean Sea that Thomas More had described earlier in *Utopia*. Their reception by friendly Indians and the temperate climate fill their ecstatic report to Raleigh. He reacts at once by dispatching a group of a hundred and eight men under Ralph Lane with explicit instructions to colonize this new land. Lane's brutality severs the Indian friendship and ends the settlement itself when the subsequent Indian reprisals force the white men back to their ships. Coincidentally, a few days later, Sir Richard Greville lands with supplies. Too late to help the settlement, he leaves behind fifteen volunteers to preserve the fort in the Queen's name.

Raleigh's enthusiasm for the project persists, despite Lane's mismanagement; for he sends out another hundred and fifty men and women in May, 1587. This band of adventurers—reduced by desertion, arguments, and sickness to a hundred and twenty-one—makes up the ill-fated Lost Colony, under the leadership of Governor John White and Ananias Dare. Principal among them, although a commoner, is John Borden who plays a major role as the events unfold. The friendship of the Indian brave, Manteo, proves inadequate in the struggle waged by the little group at Fort Raleigh. The colonists are attacked repeatedly by the warring Indians, the same tribe that had obviously killed the fifteen men left behind by Greville. Their crops are destroyed, fishing nets ripped, and outpost sentinels methodically killed by the enemy. Even worse, their hopes dim with the growing realization that Queen Elizabeth has abandoned them.

With all the odds against them, John Borden, now in command, informs Eleanor White Dare, the governor's daughter and the widow of Ananias Dare, that he has decided to accept an invitation from Manteo's people to lead the few survivors south into an unknown land called Croatoan. Eleanor confirms his decision; but, before they can discuss it with the others, a Spanish sail appears in the harbor and forces them into instant action. The starving group struggles off into the woods, shortly after Christmas, 1588; some were to be killed by the pursuing Spanish; some, by the hostile Indians; and, possibly others lived out their lives in peace with Manteo's people.

The play has two separate actions, but both are integrally connected by an overview of history. All five scenes of Act I provide a large canvas against which White's party stands out in intimate relief over the six scenes of Act II. The original expedition of Amadas and Barlowe; the primitive, religious dances of the Indians; the treachery of Lane; Raleigh's rejection of William Shakespeare as an applicant for White's adventure; the politics of Raleigh's persuasion of a reluctant Queen Elizabeth—all comprise in this first act a welter of major events and a catalogue of famous persons in history that focus in Act II on the one event of a forlorn, lost, anonymous group in forgotten Roanoke Island.

Green risked the possibility of confusing his audience with two distinct plots, but he believed that the account of Borden's final decision, and all of the sorry events leading up to it, would have little significance and credibility for a twentieth-century, sophisticated audience unless it was provided with historical background. Nor did Green intend the final effect to come from this story alone, even when the conflict literally bursts into the theater with the Indians' thirst for blood. Instead, the dramatic impact results from a combination of historic commentary and an awareness of the past as a shared experience—which occurs as the group movement, the poetic dialogue, dances, pantomime, narration, lighting and scenery, and the omnipresent music fuse into a single dimension which elicits a unified emotional response from the audience.

More than any other factor in this fusion, Green depends on the persuasiveness of music to insure audience response to *The Lost Colony*. He and Stringfield produced no new music for it, although Green did write the lyrics for a few of the songs. But the careful compilation of Elizabethan songs and hymns, and of ones with even richer tradition, gives the play a lyric, majestic quality that words and gestures alone could not have accomplished. There are thirty-one pieces in all, ranging from the well-known "Greensleeves" to Anglican liturgy hymnals that sound through the organ and chorus with overpowering force and familiarity. The organ, in fact, really binds the play more than the dialogue: it functions as a commentator in the beginning and at the end, and at the critical fourth scene of the second act when the Colony is on the brink of disaster because of Elizabeth's refusal to help. It accompanies the singing of thanksgiving in Act II, scene 3, and contrasts with the sounds of lamentation echoing Eleanor's "I know that my redeemer liveth" after the murder of Dare. The blending of the choral music with individual solo voices emphasizes the fact of man in society, and of society made up of individual, responsible men. This deep sense of community appears wistfully in the tender scene of Christmas, during the second year of the settlement, when the despairing colonists raise their tired voices in carols that had always signified peace and joy in the past.[4]

This emphasis on the people, rather than on the individual

characters, brought the sharpest criticism from even the most enthusiastic reviewers. Brooks Atkinson, for example, extolled Green's infusion of history with "a religious reverence"; but he complained that the very nature of the drama "turns his characters into unconscious symbols of a brave new world."[5] This judgment of the epic drama as a horizontal art was never disputed by Green, although his later plays did seek to reveal the inner being of his people to a greater extent. But, in *The Lost Colony,* he deliberately presents an en masse heroism of the cohesive people, and in the very same way that his audience becomes a community in his theater: people are brought together in the mutuality of their involvement on the stage and with each other. He believes that only such theater can give America an art form that contributes to and reflects the highest consciousness and aspirations of the people. The one hundred and twenty-one persons on Raleigh's mission "laughed their cryings and did their dance," but they pooled themselves into a common bond that dignified their menial tasks and insured them a place in the new compact of democracy. Green was enough of a psychologist, however, to anticipate the awkwardness of consistent mass emphasis; he singled out a few of the settlers for particular attention, particularly John Borden, Eleanor White Dare, Manteo, and Old Tom. But even in their individuality these four clear symbols of the pervasive theme of heroic democracy remain throughout Act II.

The most individualized character in the play is Old Tom. He first appears in the second scene of the first act as a beggar in the midst of Elizabethan opulence. A typical Shakespearean Fool, he is benevolently mocked by the Queen's guards; a drunkard, he is on the lookout for anyone to supply him with ale. His drinking song, after Raleigh's generous gift of a coin, rollicks with him as he rushes to the tavern; and it stays with the audience each time he appears on the stage. In the Roanoke Colony he continues as the fool, now hopelessly attached to a fat Indian squaw who considers him a newly descended god. But from this background emerges a new Tom, an appointed sentinel who is a fierce protector of the fort through the long, cold hours. His grasp of what the settlement stands for advances the theme much more than the vision of Raleigh and White, or the rhetoric of John Borden. Green intended this transformation of the Fool to be a major symbol; and, accordingly, he gave the final, significant lines of the play to Tom, who urges the disheartened band to sing out their hopes for the future.

Eleanor White Dare also undergoes change. In Elizabethan England, she is disdainful of John Borden's lower class; but, by the end of two years' experience in Roanoke, she learns that the value of men lies in their response to the challenges of life, and she thereby expunges her inherited value of nobility through blood. She gives birth to the first child born in Roanoke, suffers the death of her husband, and links thereby the eternal process of birth and death; but she does so only in a passive role. In her love for John Borden, however, she actively renews the birth symbol. Her coming alive again through him signifies the overall theme of the play—death cannot overcome the man possessed by a dream. Through her reversal and her heroic reaction, along with other examples throughout the play, Green includes the great and small for heroic possibility. Just as he removes from Old Tom the blemish of his past indignities, so he drops from Eleanor the aristocratic prejudice that would prevent the fulfillment of her personality. Her completion comes when she, the aristocrat, and John Borden, the commoner, join in loving relationship.

John Borden, unlike Tom and Eleanor, never changes and, thus, is not so successfully drawn for the stage. Early in the play, when the rascally Captain Fernando rails against the projected trip to the New World, Borden accuses him of selling out to Spain. He then challenges the people to undergo the voyage of great peril as proof of their national pride. His position is sound, of course, for the group's lagging spirits need support. But his clairvoyance and correct stance, here and throughout the drama, obviate the possibility of tragic human error. They also pose the most menial tasks and innocuous events against a panoramic backdrop of history, a projection which cancels out the human element. Perhaps the best example of this is the expression of Borden's love to Eleanor. Their conversation on the night before the fated emigration to Croatoan spells out his deepest feelings for her but hardly in a passionate outburst. Instead, his love and desire are intimately related to the success of Raleigh's mission.

Borden's tenacity and steady resolution are admirable, but the audience suspects that John must have his own doubts as one plan after another fails; he must despise the Crown that has obviously defected in its responsibility; he must hate the savage Indians and be impatient with others who lack his endurance and vision. Yet only his irrevocable determination appears, and he works always for others rather than for himself. Such self-possession is magnified to epical proportions, but in no way does it identify an audience with him, except in the form of worship; for John is too far above for the ordinary man to know him. He is less a person and more the abstraction—the spirit of America.

In this deliberate dissolution of individual concern for the greater one of the common good, Green includes all of mankind against a cosmic background. Thus, he presents as early as the second scene the primitive rites of the Indians. When the medicine man, Uppowoc, prays to his god for protection of his people, the Indians become part of the universal family under God. Their ritual to the corn god differs only in form from the Christian rites at the Christmas and baptism scenes. They are seen in peace and as not naturally savage. When their ritual ends abruptly with the sounds of the English horn and gun, the outside threats to the Indian security are posed in the same way that the dynamite blasts signaled the end of peace for the Negroes in *Potter's Field*. Accordingly, Captain Lane's slaughter of so many Indians, and of Chief Wingina particularly, justifies the Indian massacre of the white settlers thereafter. Green could not stress this aspect of justice without blurring his focus on the white settlers. Nevertheless, by implication, including Wachese and Manteo and the other Indians on the side of justice, he echoes the words he gave to Gilchrist earlier in *The Field God*—"deep down people ain't Christian, Jew or Gentile, black or white, but just people."

The first scene of *The Lost Colony*, actually a Prologue, includes almost all of the elements that constitute the epic drama. The spoken word joins the hymn of praise to God's power, as the organ thunders it over the countryside. A minister asks the audience to witness how God's grace sanctified this holy spot with the heroic deeds of the people who settled there three centuries before. The chorus booms out its praise of God's grace that was made manifest in these famed and unknown English pioneers who followed their collective dream, who made their lives significant in a search for the grail. The minister responds that the dream still lives in the minds and hearts of those in Manteo tonight who honor the memories of their forebears; that, in fact, the grail awaits new seekers. The chorus fades out with a final praise to God as the lights focus on the historian who sets the drama into motion.

Without any forced persuasion, this prologue prepares the audience for the ensuing action through the antiphonal exchange between the minister and the chorus, both of whom are in awe of the events already known to them. The dream and the shrine aspects, in turn, signify the abstract qualities of the ideal, a perfection which remains untranslatable and unfelt when expressed in mere words. The reverential and overpowering organ and choral music, however, translates them into emotional forces which render the audience impressed and believing. Other elements conjoin as the play unfolds.

But in this evocation of a common mood, one which is prompted by an emotional sense of the past, Green lays the groundwork for all of the symphonic dramas he was to write thereafter. The plots and the characters do change; and the different techniques brought to each new play strengthen or weaken the effect. But Green never departed from this drawing in of his audience to a sacred meeting where they could enlarge their vision to include the cosmic nature of heroism. Anything else that occurs during the performances is only incidental.

The movement and the theme of the play are actually one, and depend on the narrator who fuses time and space and opens the audience to the cosmic dimensions of human activity. Before the tragic fate of the Lost Colony can be experienced, the historian sets the colonists' activities against the original expeditions so that the later voyage will not appear as an isolated incident. Thus, Raleigh's dream, an isolated act, propels into action Amadus and Barlow, whose immediate exultant triumph ends in the later disaster of fifteen men left behind, isolated and presumed killed by the Indians. So, too, the second migration under John White starts out at Raleigh's command, an en masse venture that dissolves into a few scattered, isolated men and women, symbolized in Borden and Eleanor. The parallel events depend upon each other, and add a larger dimension of grandeur to the story of the Lost Colony. In contrast, the fifteen men, lost after Greville departed for assistance, disappear as only impersonal items in a registry, or as a footnote to history, different from the lost ones following Borden into the woods, brought alive onto Green's stage.

Green looks into the dry, musty pages and finds, out of his imaginative recreation, the heroic assertion that gives his characters dramatic vibrancy. On the night before their departure from Plymouth, for example, Eleanor replies to Raleigh's wonder over her wish to go with the group: "I only know day and night that I feel this narrow England and hear the call of the unknown world sounding in my ear. I do, Sir Walter, like you I do." In an identical situation, on the night before they are to brave the paths to Croatoan, "into the vast unknown, out of sight forever," John and Eleanor express again their determination to bring their dream to an end in a peaceful, free Fort Raleigh, when they return at a later date. Such dreams are the stuff of greatness. Such heroes are the makers of new worlds; resilient in defeat, prophetic in vision, they are also models for succeeding generations.

CHAPTER 8

Additional European Explorations

I The Highland Call

BEFORE *The Lost Colony*, many successful pageants had been produced in different sections of the country: George Pierce Baker's *Control: A Pageant of Engineering Progress*, in 1930, at Hoboken, New Jersey; Sidney Howard's *Lexington*, in 1925, written for Lexington, Massachusetts; Stevens' and Mackaye's *Pageant and Masque of St. Louis*, in 1914; Thomas Wood Stevens' *The Pageant of Virginia*, in 1922; Koch's masque on Raleigh, already mentioned; and many others. All of them concentrated on a clearly enunciated theme peculiar to the community or locale that sponsored the production. This theme or idea dominated the agents involved, so that the pageant became an abstraction no different from the medieval spectacles that moved about the market place on carts. A sense of community pride was effected through the depiction of historic events—rather than characters or persons—and through incidental music, dance, and mass movement.

Green knew of the success of men like Percy Mackaye and Thomas Wood Stevens in this art form; but, when he came to write the Roanoke celebration, he was unwilling to follow the pattern available to him. Instead, he utilized the stylized elements of music and dance of the pageant only as they could add dimension to the drama. The story, before all other things, with its concentration on character and emotional response, distinguished Green's departure from the traditional pageant. Because of his shift to a radical, unfamiliar form, Green was unsure of the audience reaction before the opening and during the first slow two weeks of *The Lost Colony*. But, after the word circulated about the unusual event on Roanoke Island and after the crowds flocked to the Waterside Theater by the thousands, Green knew that "this sort of drama was exactly fitted to the needs and dramatic genius of the American people." Although he wrote a few things in other forms over the subsequent years —*The Enchanted Maze* in 1939, *Native Son* in 1941, *Dog on the Sun* in 1949, and numerous essays and one-act plays—Green's artistic commitment after *The Lost Colony* was almost totally to this kind of drama, a medium which he believes will ultimately be indigenous to American culture more than anything that comes out of commercial theater anywhere.

Green's success brought an immediate invitation to write a symphonic drama celebrating the first Scots' settlement in the Cape Fear Valley. Aside from a desire to continue in this exciting new medium, Green accepted out of a fierce pride for the valley and for his own Harnett County, which had become Little Bethel in his folk stories and plays. The drama he wrote— *The Highland Call*—arose from the legends and tales familiar to him from childhood and from an abiding interest in the European founders of the country. As such, this drama formed a sequel to *The Lost Colony,* in that it dramatized European colonization of the New World, again under English hegemony. Unlike the previous play, it was performed indoors by the Carolina Playmakers at the Lafayette Opera House from November 20 through November 24, 1939. Although it had an emotional appeal for the local people, the play ran its course quickly because of its limited subject matter but also because of concern over the impending war.

The play tells of the great MacDonald clan, lords of the Western Isles, who migrate to vast lands of Carolina, ceded to them by the Crown in 1774. Instead of furthering the new democracy sweeping through the country, their leaders attempt only to extend the realm of the British Crown. Their main spokesman, Flora MacDonald, calls out great rallying cries for unity, in words that attest to her sincerity, but which show her to be completely out of date. The peace she longs for rests on a continued stratification of classes, a distinction that obviates any love affair between her niece, Peggy MacNeil, and her bonded servant, Dan Murchison. Since Flora's social values do not obtain in the New World, Dan, at the end of his indenture, fights with the Whigs to defeat the Highland Brigade and then offers his hand in marriage to Peggy. When she accepts, the old and

Additional European Explorations

the new join in a ritual of democracy that includes the great and the lowly. But Flora refuses defeat, and she returns to Scotland rather than take the North Carolina Assembly vote of allegiance.[1]

Green continued here the formula that had succeeded with *The Lost Colony*: he projected the Carolina insurrection against a larger canvas of the English-Scottish wars. In turn, he took the struggles in the North to form a Continental Congress and the battles of Lexington, Bunker Hill, and Montreal, and filtered them down into the personal lives of the lovers. The formula failed, however, because the main characters never took on personality. Flora is a pompous caricature, static in vision and rhetorical in speech. She fixes her eye on a dream and loses reality as she ignores experience and relationships. Nor are Dan and Peggy, as the spokesmen of youth and a new world, anything more than the tracings of an ideal greater than themselves. Had Flora disappeared in the play as a vague abstraction, and had Dan replaced her as a flesh-and-blood hero, the action might have been believable, or interesting. Instead, the drama is little more than a circumscribed series of events involving the principal characters in lengthy arguments over the cause of liberty.

Flora and Dan, then, however vague they are, are in this tragic moment of history the center around whom all the other people move. But, unlike *The Lost Colony*, the movement never develops into any ritual mass significance. Aside from inadequate character delineation, as suggested before, the physical limitations of the Opera House restricted the author to a narration of battles, to fewer episodes than he was allowed on the Roanoke triple stage, and to less spectacle and group arrangements. There are some excellent scenes in the play, nevertheless. A grand entrance of the MacDonalds in the second scene has all the splash of an Elizabethan court procession. The clashes between a few isolated Liberty Boys and young Tories produce the excitement of a mob frenzy. A festive Highland Reel in the second act adds interest and also diverts attention from the impending catastrophe.

Perhaps the best element of this drama is the music. Green selected fifty-one old Scotch songs, ballads, dances, and hymns —many of them peculiar to the Cape Fear Valley Scots—and distributed them between the chorus and the solo voices. Again he used the organ for sonorous effects, in this case through Charles Vardell's creative overture which picked up fragments of the many Scottish tunes. The organ in the very beginning skirls out bagpipe notes; shifts into an old hymn, "St. Anne's"; tolls out the dead march from "The Highland Widow's Lament"; and ends with the thematic music which identifies Flora MacDonald throughout the play. Like a vast echo, the chorus sings out the "Flora MacDonald Lament" and sets the mood of the whole play, which culminates in the swell of the rising organ chords in the final scene as a broken Flora leaves for Scotland. From the opening wail of the bagpipe notes on the organ, through "Barbara Allen," and "Scots Ha'e Wi' Wallace Bled," to the final organ reprise, Green blends hymn tunes, folk songs, and ballads into a total Scottish suite—the most successfully integrated element of the entire play.

In *The Highland Call*, Green sanctified the soil of the drama's setting; or, more precisely, the work took its final meaning from the sacred place, as another "shrine drama." In it, he pursued one major idea—the theme that occupied him throughout his entire career: the importance of the freedom of contemporary man which grew out of a struggle that his forefathers had endured. This struggle was an anguish that pitted members of families against each other and demanded "heart-breaking decisions on hard facts that must replace empty dreams." Discovery of these facts of history, emotionally realized, reminds the audience of its own indifference, or, at least, awakens it to values and ideals once known but now forgotten. The difficulty with this play, however, is that they will soon be forgotten: the idea emerges in heavily attired rhetoric instead of in memorable human action at a critical moment of history.

In *The Highland Call*, the historic context, the honorific ideas on liberty, and the ever-present music combined effectively to add immeasurable quality to the Fayetteville celebration. But the drama also needed vital human conflict in dramatic terms to be successful theater for all time. After the great effect of *The Lost Colony*, this second symphonic drama in no way suggested that Green could repeat his first success.

II *The Founders*

Paul Green wrote other and more successful symphonic dramas than *The Highland Call* before he resumed the subject of European colonization of America. The earlier dramas in-

Additional European Explorations

clude *The Common Glory, Faith of Our Fathers,* and *Wilderness Road* and they will be discussed in the following chapter as part of the theme of the building of America. However, the lesson of conquest in peace taught by the early explorers held his interest over the major part of his life, both as history and as exemplary action for twentieth century men. The events at Jamestown in the first years of the seventeenth century, accordingly, were ready-made for *The Founders,* which he wrote for a production in 1957 to celebrate the three hundred and fiftieth anniversary of the settlement of the English colony.

In Green's mind, the Jamestown material worked directly out of the events he had dramatized for *The Lost Colony.* Sometime after John Borden led his stragglers off to Croatoan in 1587, Sir Walter Raleigh turned away from the New World when he gave all of his holdings to Sir Thomas Smith and the other stockholders of the Virginia Company. Smith thereafter dispatched three ships, with a hundred and forty-three people in 1607. Despite years of starvation and harassment from the Indians, additional pilgrims were sent to reinforce the settlement. This policy, coupled with extraordinary human endurance by the settlers, led to the ultimate success realized in the first legislative assembly in Jamestown in 1619—the very thing that White, Dare, and Borden had dreamed of in their abortive experiment. But, aside from the sequential historic material, Green found in the men and in the events dramatic substance of great appeal for modern audiences.

The original plan for *The Founders* called for an amphitheater on the Jamestown site. But the producers experienced something of the early hardships suffered there when water problems in the swampy areas forced a shift to Williamsburg, where the Cove Amphitheater was constructed specifically for this play.[2] Green used the natural background of rocks, water, hedges, trees, and sky to such an extent that the early performances took place in the late afternoon so that he could use the sunlight as an integral element. The amphitheater enabled Green to fashion his material on a larger canvas than the one he had used for *The Highland Call.* Like his first play at Roanoke, the action literally occurs in the Jamestown settlement, with the structures cut away for audience visibility, and set against Lake Matoaka for egress to the English ships. The swift movement of the people, the time gaps, and the interchange and altercations between the settlers and the Indians forced the author to find technical solutions through playlets in hinted action in pantomime, and in ritual group movements. While the large stage enabled such a fusion, a reading of the play adds nothing to Green's reputation; it indicates how *The Founders,* perhaps more than any other work of Green's, must be seen to be appreciated.

The play covers a period from 1607 through 1619, but the heroism of John Rolfe and Pocahontas carries the final import of Jamestown's success. The action also includes the earlier unsuccessful attempts by John Smith to effect a concordance with King Powhatan, and the martial tyranny of Governor Thomas Dale that paradoxically solidifies the colony's defenses. Rolfe's joy over the legislative assembly and the appointment of Governor Yeardley in 1619 ends abruptly when he is killed in a sudden Indian attack. His death sums up the woes of all the settlers over the long span, but the official funeral ceremony indicates even more the binding force his death gives to the community.

In his previous music dramas, Green had made use of the narrator at the opening of the play to set the historic scene and to establish with the music a mood proper to the unfolding events. But in *The Founders* he compels immediate attention by plunging at once into a pantomime reaction of an Indian tribe at the sight and sound of an English ship. Immediately before this opening, the organ music poses a conflict with the heavy chords of the "Huguenot Battle Hymn" mixed with more subtle Indian sounds. At the same time, a drum beats ominously and a hunting horn sounds in the distance. As a kind of echo, the entering chorus, made up of the settlers themselves, rather than a group of singers offstage, sing with joyous abandon "The Huguenot Hymn." Their naiveté sets the mood for the entire first act, in that their excitement about setting foot on land after the long sea voyage exposes them to Indian cunning and annihilation.

The whole first act dictates this lesson of preparedness to the explorers, one that John Smith had tried to teach them before without success. They fail to learn, and so the act ends with the full circle reached when the pioneers depart in defeat, once again under the hidden eyes of the Indians. The first act, which remains on the level of pageantry, sets the scene for the second act with massive strokes of historic matter for the emergence of drama in the persons of Rolfe and Pocahontas. It poses men caught in the trap of hostile nature and unfriendly Indians, torn

Additional European Explorations

apart by internecine quarrels, and on the brink of defeat; the turn of events comes with the appearance of John Rolfe in the second act.

When Green researched material for the substance of his drama, he could not discover a proper hero in history's favorite, Captain John Smith, nor in Christopher Newport, Thomas Dale, William Berkeley, nor Governor Yeardley. Instead, he gleaned from his reading the outline of John Rolfe, a commoner who arrived at the colony in 1610 in the middle of the worst period of starvation, and who infused the others with a new spirit of hope that carried them through to victory. In addition, his disdain of gold and his cultivation of tobacco ultimately provided the moral sustenance and economic leverage necessary for survival. His gentle relations with all and his marriage to Princess Pocahontas completed the history and the character of this early democrat.

Green's Rolfe, unfortunately, never fills in this outline. He remains one-dimensional: earthy in limited desires, plain in language, and simplistic in his approach to all problems. Thus, he sees the hostile Indians as only naughty children. He submerges his love for Pocahontas beneath the more important mission of the colony. He never doubts his own competence in the face of overwhelming odds. Altogether, his self-assurance and emotionless actions distance him from an uncaring audience.

Despite this oversized hero and an obviously thin plot, *The Founders* realistically translated to the stage the few joys and enormous sorrows of all those who lived in this bitter period of history. The courage and endurance of these men and women are feelingly expressed in short poignant dialogues and vignettes that cover the starvation period of 1609-10, at the same time that the colonists are shown in their animal drives for food. Their confidence in God's providential control of their mission rings out in their singing of "Hymn in Time of Storm" and "O Lord, in Thee Is All My Trust." Their community ties rollick in drinking songs and tunes for dancing. The shouting and laughter, and the heavy but healthy sexual byplay, close out for a little while the shadow of death. The dance and the music here, and throughout the rest of the play, spring out of the characters in the action of the moment: such an incongruous affair of all the women picking their men for husbands would have to be one of wild abandon, fear, and joy. The sense of community shared develops further as all the players observe the grace and love in the marriage of Rolfe and Pocahontas, and it culminates when all solemnly mourn Rolfe's death as a generous sacrifice for the colony.

Green's attempt to dramatize the love affair of Rolfe and Pocahontas and to present them as archetypal mother and father of America fails to involve the audience on an intimate level. Perhaps twentieth-century audiences are too sophisticated, or jaded, to accept life arranged in such simple, consistent patterns. But, even if these two historic figures never emerge as identifiable human beings, *The Founders* manages to dissolve time and dispositions and to serve as a medium for a more cosmic emotional identification with the men of the past who suffered the harrowing days of the foundation of America. As such, like *The Lost Colony*, it is a vital part of the nation, critical history unfolded in intense dramatic terms.

III *Cross and Sword*

In 1937, Brooks Atkinson praised Green's imaginative flair and poetic expression in *The Lost Colony*, but he warned that "pageantry is horizontal art; drama is vertical, ranging from the inner life of the private man to the empyrean of human aspiration."[3] Certain aspects of the early symphonic dramas clearly fell within this judgment and warning; for Green's group concentration, as noted earlier, was deliberate. To offset a total mass effect, individual characters were invented for dramatic and philosophical emphasis; but, although John Borden, Dan Murchison, and John Rolfe prevent the plays from fragmenting into unconnected episodes, they hardly emerge as clearly recognizable persons. One of their serious limitations is their talk, which is designedly more declamatory than conversational. Atkinson's complaint, however, does not apply to the next play to be discussed. *Cross and Sword*, in which the author successfully related the dance, music, pantomime, and other elements of spectacle for a "vertical" delineation of the main character.

This play took Green into the seventeenth-century period of Spanish dominance in Florida and other Southern states; and it was his fourth and last study of European exploration in the New World. It opened on June 27, 1965, as the main attraction of St. Augustine's four hundredth anniversary; and it was played in

Additional European Explorations

an amphitheater constructed for it in Anastasia State Park. Governor Haydon Burns and past Governor Farris Bryant honored the premiere, along with two thousand others who sat in an arena made of coquina, the native stone that had been used in the first Spanish fort in Anastasia. After that night, attendance was consistently high for five seasons; and *Cross and Sword* has become an annual event in this northern Florida city.

Cross and Sword tells of the expedition of Pedro Menendez De Aviles, a captain general sent by Philip II to colonize Florida and to convert the Indians. The Spanish explorers before him had failed, in that no permanency obtained in this new territory, suddenly made invaluable with the discovery of gold in 1530. No mission was more wasted, for example, than that of Ponce de Leon, whose confusion of Florida for the island of Bimini brought him no closer to a Fountain of Youth, nor to a durable settlement that would return the investment of his time, men, and his king's money. Nor did Cabeza de Vaca, Hernando de Soto, or Francisco de Coronado do anything more than carelessly explore the vast territory and make random claims. Not until August 28, 1565—the feast day of Saint Augustine—did Spain proclaim herself ruler of all of the new land, by reason of the actual settlement of her people in Florida under the governorship of Menendez. Against this background of historic adventure, Green dramatizes Menendez' story.

The play opens with the landing of the colonists in the New World. Menendez immediately solidifies his newly established colony of St. Augustine when he defeats Jean Ribaut, the captain of the French colony at Fort Caroline, and effects peaceful relations with Oriba, the king of the Indian tribe there. Menendez faces a dilemma thereafter as a married Christian and as protector of his people when Oriba offers to him his sister, Notina, as a token of peace. In a delaying action, Menendez sends her to Havana to be reared as a Christian lady. Furious over the obvious rejection of his gift, Oriba lays siege to the fort and cuts off all access to food. At this point, Menendez faces the hard decision that every tragic hero must resolve. He opposes war yet obviously must defend his people and the Spanish Crown. He can do so by marriage to Notina, but thereby damn his soul through polygamy. He decides to make a sinful marriage, out of love for her, and also to prevent the inevitable battle with the Indians. But Notina, recently returned as a Christian from

Havana, refuses his offer and its consequent damnation of the soul. She suggests, instead, that he raid the Indians, no longer her people, for the needed food. He agrees after further soul-searching, quickly routs the Indian forces, and brings back supplies to the colony. He successfully repulses a counterattack, but Notina is killed while defending him. The play ends shortly after, with Menendez' farewell to St. Augustine as he leaves for Spain to report to his king.

In the same way that Johnny Johnson and Abe McCranie control characters and events in their plays, so does Menendez dominate *Cross and Sword*. In the new colony, unlike the Spanish stereotype, he opts for peace rather than war: when the peace is not forthcoming, he shoulders the responsibility for failure. He performs physical labors double that of the average man. He anguishes over the feelings of a native girl whereas previous conquistadors had coupled with the women without any scruples. The audience comes to know him in this inner struggle to resolve the problem of Notina. Green has him respond in a seemingly contradictory way as any man in love would do: "falling into sin" at the same time that he offers up his moral failure for the safety of St. Augustine. This complexity of motive adds life to the play, so that the history-making foundation of the colony actually results from one man's troubled spirit. Green had written history with a societal compassion in the previous symphonic dramas, but in *Cross and Sword* he probed the inner dynamics of his hero to produce deep emotional effects.

Green also worked for these effects through an infusion of life into the minor characters. Unfortunately, Notina, the most important of them, resisted such treatment: she is another Pocahontas, a creature of love who symbolically bridges the primitive and cultivated civilizations. Even in her sophisticated gesture to save Menendez from adultery, her decision comes from one who may have been changed in Havana but not to the audience's knowledge. The sacrifice that each of the lovers makes has the stuff of drama in it, but hers lacks the complexity of Menendez'. Hers is only the expected Christian moral response to the temptation of sin, one which tells something of the penny catechism, but nothing of her deeper self.

The character of Albarez is more successfully drawn and is, therefore, one of the better miniatures produced in these epic-dramas. Albarez is a Paul Green man, another soldier whose ambition is to fill a role in peace, in this case as a builder or as an architect. Reticent in speech, his feelings and commitment run deep and are lasting. His moral strength approximates the quality that enabled Hardy Gilchrist to remain his own man. Thus, when Eva remarks that the supplies will come from Spain if only the colonists pray hard enough, he answers, "You pray, and I will keep my soldiers and muskets ready. . . ." Like Menendez, he also has a softer side: when a few of his soldiers mutiny, he quells the uprising, forgives the men, and chooses not to inform on them to the commander. In plays like this one, where the mass movement tends to diminish the individual, Albarez, like Menendez, stands out. Indeed, if Menendez had not been on the scene, Albarez would have been the hero.

This delineation of character is built out of the material of ordinary drama but, even more, from the added dimensions of music, dance, and group action, and from the other devices that Green uses in the symphonic dramas. The play would be empty without music, just as the absence of it in Menendez' life would be unendurable for him. The whole first scene indicates how major the role of music will be throughout. The sonorous swell of the organ, mixed with piped voices, fills the amphitheater in a majestic hymn to God the Father Almighty. This hymn echoes at the beginning of the second act, and at the very end of the play; it stitches the entire movement from Spain to the New World into an integrated whole. The largo music that personalizes Menendez' dream in the first scene slips off into eerie sounds from the same flute, violin, and guitar to achieve the weird effect of de Leon's search for the Fountain of Youth. This largo has a faint echo in the love lyric that is sung by an unseen Frenchman on the night before the bloody battle between Ribaut and Menendez. This lyric in turn, which sets the scene for Menendez' concern for his troops before battle, like "a little touch o' Harry in the night," has its own reprise in Menendez' second dream at the end of the first act. The music springs out of the action, or subtly comments on and anticipates it throughout the play. Thus, the song by the women at work in the last scene of the first act has the intensity and swiftness of the palmetto thatching that involves them as they sing; and it achieves this effect in the same appropriate way that the royal music sets the scene for King Philip's commission to Menendez in Act I, scene 2.

Before the production was under way, the director, L. I. Zimmerman, persuaded Green to a less realistic interpretation of his script. He argued that a futuristic setting of free forms, sharp angles and planes, and more imaginative lighting would open the play to the fuller possibilities that Green had always hoped for in symphonic drama. The results proved Zimmerman correct; for, with sixteen different levels on the three stages, the union of dance and group movement of the hundred-odd cast with the music and spoken words of the play is remarkable. Instead of the traditional wind machines and thunder sheets for storms, the hurricane scene in the play, immediately before Menendez' trip to Havana, is achieved through dancers wheeling across the stage to simulate the intense winds and rains. The gathering of the coquina for the houses, the Christian teaching of the Indians, and Menendez' grueling march and attack on Ribaut are similarly choreographed as complete vignettes. The highly flexible stage allowed for the ritual Indian mating dance for Notina, and for the grimmer war dance toward the end of the play. The use of skrims to project the dreams allowed the audience to see de Leon portrayed on the stage, instead of being told about him in a narrative flashback. It also translated Menendez' anxieties into real images beyond anything that words alone could have done. The use of Basilio Bonito as a settler with his own personal problems, as father of the first child born in America, as comic relief, and also as an occasional narrator integrated the narration and action in the same way that the music and dance evolved naturally out of the situation. *Cross and Sword* marks a high point in Green's long involvement with this art form that began where the pageant ended.

These four symphonic dramas, *The Lost Colony,* *The Highland Call, The Founders,* and *Cross and Sword* complete Paul Green's reverential treatment of the motives and deeds of the explorers who carried Europe's civilization to an entirely new land. His entire approach to the subject matter rests on the premise that a moral weariness, or a corruption in the old country, brought on by centuries of class structure, deprived the majority of their free rights, a corruption which arose from a corresponding removal of the ruling class from the soil. In the New World, the English, Scot, and Spanish settler felt a power emanating from the land and from his own industry which made him the equal of a king. Like Whitman, Green insists in these plays that a mystical transformation takes place when a man establishes himself in America. Like Colonel McAllister in *The Highland Call*, he is moved by something greater than himself. This mysterious flowing grace, pouring in abundance on America, underlies this country's apprehension of universal liberty, freedom, and justice: it is the source for her laws, government, and practical democracy. Also like Whitman, Green traced the different aspects of that government and democracy in his writings, but nowhere more effectively than in his symphonic dramas about America's discovery and growth.

CHAPTER *9*

Laying the Foundation of America

I *The Common Glory*

THE GUGGENHEIM that Green received in 1928 enabled him to see Europe under better conditions than did his first trip which ended in muddy trenches. He was introduced to vast areas outside "Little Bethel" country, where values were not determined by a "made-in-America" tag. His rich experience as a Rockefeller lecturer in Asia in 1951 and his other trips to Paris, Greece, and Russia, which complemented prolific reading of the great writers of other cultures, equipped him with a world view as subtle and sophisticated as anyone's in the State Department. His consistent support of the United Nations since its inception placed him in square opposition to isolationists and provincials who cried "My country right or wrong." Even so, after the success of *The Lost Colony*, Green never sought beyond America for subject matter.[1] With each new period of research for the symphonic dramas, he concluded that America uniquely provides the chance for a man to fulfill himself in peace and happiness.

Green brought to his subject matter a kind of biblical aura, a confidence in a New Jerusalem America; but he also grieved over the racism, poverty, and chauvinism that threatened the great American experiment in living. He insists in his works that the men and women of early history who faced challenges that were fundamentally no different from contemporary problems, survived and triumphed in many cases, because their confidence in God and a mutuality with their fellow men finally produced a united government of thirteen little Europes. On the other hand, Green's insistence on individual responsibility does

Laying the Foundation of America

not demand blind loyalty. On numerous occasions, he vigorously opposed the government's position—federal, state, or village. He believes also that America's destiny lies in an established harmony with the other nations of the world, but one which must be worked at night and day, one which requires eternal vigilance by every involved member. It is no wonder that his ideal in political theory and action has been from the very beginning, Thomas Jefferson's.

Long before Green actually used the person of Jefferson as the subject for a play, this "key to Jeffersonian philosophy" appeared in Abe McCranie's undelivered speech to the school board in *In Abraham's Bosom;* in Hardy Gilchrist's protest against the community tyranny over his morals and religion in *The Field God;* in numerous plays and short stories where the central figure must work at the endless problems of the common good and personal freedom. In them all, before all other considerations, the steady Jeffersonian line of the individual as the absolute unit appears as a dominant thought.

After *The Lost Colony* had completed its third successful year, and *The Highland Call* properly celebrated the Scots' first settlement in the Cape Fear Valley, Green himself suggested in 1939 that the eighteenth-century Georgian perfection of Williamsburg seemed correct for a play along the lines he had produced at Roanoke; in fact, the area was the "shrined" birthplace of American freedom. When he was commissioned to write the play, he actually started what turned out to be *The Founders,* which was produced many years later in 1957, as described above. The impending war ended the plans abruptly, so that the play about Jefferson actually did not appear until 1947. When it did, Thomas Jefferson and the making of the American nation became the subject, instead of the original one of John Rolfe and the founding of Jamestown. Even more than the community involvement in the play at Roanoke ten years before, this play, *The Common Glory,* required the participation by every little town and large city in the state of Virginia: assessments spread throughout the state to provide funds for capital expenditures. The play opened on July 17, 1947, in the Lake Matoaka Amphitheater, built expressly for the play, under the aegis of the Jamestown Corporation.

In this first symphonic drama about the building of America, Green faced a different challenge. In his previous plays, John

Borden and Dan Murchison were free of the limitations of historic facts imposed on the character of Jefferson. In them, too, Green wrote his own plays for whatever esthetic effect he desired and, in turn, for the kind of audience his play would seek. But in *The Common Glory*, the Jamestown Corporation insisted on a play to delight mature audiences at the same time that it would please and instruct the thousands of children who would come from distant points to Williamsburg. A third problem was for Green to make Jefferson a real human being, and one in no way offensive to the very large Jefferson cult in Virginia. That he succeeded in meeting this challenge can be seen in the fact that the play has a record of performance that places it second to *The Lost Colony*.

The Common Glory, which covers a period between 1774 and 1781, tells of Thomas Jefferson's involvement in the Continental Congress; in the writing of the Declaration of Independence at Philadelphia; in the defense of George Washington against the states' rightists of the Virginia Assembly; in fruitless argument for religious freedom and an end to slavery; in the rallying of flagging spirits during the American Revolution; and in the personal tragedy of his wife's sickness and death. Jefferson actually comes to life in the second act, when the audience shares the anguish of his decisions and of the loss of his wife. By then, Virginia has declared herself an enemy of King George and has actually sent money to the north to General Washington. Even more so than Patrick Henry, the ailing governor and military leader of Virginia, in the development of the play Jefferson has assumed the responsibility of his state's commitment and has struggled on every level to push the colonial army to success. In this first scene,[2] he sags over a desk in the governor's palace in Williamsburg, exhausted from his endless burdens. The time is Green's favorite one for exploring his characters in high and low moods: the sentimental period of Christmas.

Jefferson's inner self appears in his intimate relationships: with his widowed sister Martha; with his household Negro mammy, Aunt Nancy; with his scholarly tutor, George Wythe; and particularly with his wife, Patty. With all four, he sloughs off the responsibility of public care and relaxes into the gentle, compassionate, meditative, sentimental person of Monticello. He even appears as the lover in the lyric that he and Patty sing, "Now what is love, I pray thee fain." He cannot rid his thoughts of the war, but even this admixture of national need and personal wishes gives Jefferson dimension. His failure to comprehend Patty's meaning when she tries to tell him of her coming death makes him fallible but human, particularly since the audience knows him in history only as a supremely intelligent man. In addition, the hint of his wife's death coalesces the hero's impending personal tragedy with his efforts to father a new nation. The scene promotes additional understanding of Jefferson as a person and of the role he played in history when a delegation from the Virginia Assembly forces itself upon him in his home to insist that he withdraw Virginia's troops. The scene successfully fuses Jefferson's faith and total involvement in the Revolution with his intense love for Patty, and it anticipates in the personal and the colonial aspects, strong possibility of failure and loss.[3]

The third scene of this second act provides another view of Jefferson the man. Like the Christmas scene, it is a favorite part of any play where Green presents a hero: Jefferson appears at the Jamestown Fort but too late to suppress an open rebellion of starving soldiers. His friend, Captain Hugh Taylor, had just tried in vain to check them; but now, even he has lost all hope in the Revolution. Hugh sees the people, "swapping and buying and trading in the life blood of us poor fools who have gone forth to die on the battlefield," and Congress as no better in its squabbling and mean considerations. Jefferson responds that he knows of his predecessors' rape of the Indians and black men, of congressional petty concerns, and of the average man's selfishness. But, beyond all that, there began in this area an idea of freedom that cannot be expunged; a formula for democracy was conceived that would end forever such acts of inhumanity.

As a rallying speech for the masses, this rhetoric might do. But Green uses the language ironically to probe Jefferson, who now feels the ebb of his strength and who wonders over the justice of the violence that has uprooted families, destroyed homes, and "brought forth murder and rapine and pillage and the muck and filth and horror of destruction." Now he questions if the people are ready for democracy, or if he really believes in the truth of his own past words. By such irresolution this great man of history moves out of legend into humanity. Epical heroes, like Achilles and Beowulf, for all of their seemingly insurmountable hazards, never consider the possibility of failure. But Green gives Jefferson human stature, not epical dimension, particularly in this scene after his talk with Hugh.

Paradoxically, however, Jefferson is the collective hero. The first act, for example, explicates the historic background of the Revolution, including the opposing views of King George and William Pitt, the internecine fights of the colonists themselves, and the philosophic schema of the Declaration of Independence. These are moments and figures of great import, and the audience is carried by them into the current of epochal movement, but they do not contribute to the dramatic enlargement of Jefferson's character. He is only a part of it all, important in his rebellious stance and strength. He is a visionary in his conception of freedom spelled out in law and human action, but he is not altogether a fully realized person on the stage. Nor do the two scenes save him from this archetypal role, for they come too late, and are followed by three scenes in which he becomes the leader again, once more the rallier of the people with his powerful rhetoric. Not that this constitutes a major flaw in the play; on the contrary, the two intimate glimpses blend with the oversized figure to produce an effect that teases and impresses. The major difficulty that the playwright faced in satisfying the Jefferson cult—in conforming to the facts of history and yet creating a real person—was met by having the hero operate on both the personal and national level. Confined as he was by so many prescriptions, Green drew a remarkable portrait of Thomas Jefferson.

The play itself takes on greater humanity, however, through the minor characters, particularly Hugh Taylor and Cephus Sicklemore. Hugh carries forward the theme of the "common glory" more so than Jefferson, for he is a tenant farmer, only recently out of bondage. Like John Borden and Dan Murchison, he is prepared to give his life for freedom. Green bends history to this dramatic purpose by attributing to him the final phrase of the Declaration of Independence, although Taylor never saw it in a larger, philosophic context. An attempt to flesh the character of Taylor through a love affair with Eileen Gordon, the daughter of the Tory leader, fails because it is overwhelmed by the major events and themes of the play. The relationship, however, does show Green's inventiveness in Eileen. She holds her father's political beliefs steadily, so that she insists upon Hugh's love carrying with it a promise to assist her father.

In contrast to Eileen, the two young girls in *The Lost Colony* and in *The Highland Call* easily take on new values of democracy with love for Borden and Murchison, because their standards had never been examined, and because they are less complex women. But Eileen's position is a thoughtful one, almost unfeminine, compared with the girls in the other plays. Like Cordelia, in *King Lear* she knows the love proper for lover and for father, and both must be honored. Had Eileen been given greater attention by the author, she would have been the most interesting person in the play. Moreover, she does not misplace her loyalty and respect. Her father is no villain but an aristocrat like Flora MacDonald whose faith in England never flags: "still her glory, her greatness, her ideals of liberty, of justice shall continue." Even in the burning of his house, in his ill-tempered railing against Jefferson, and in his suicide after Yorktown, he appears in dignity. Like so many others in uncertain times, he fails to see history in its unfolding and so throws all of his energies into the wrong cause.

But it is Cephus Sicklemore, "a man of words and no property," who brings real humanity to the play, even in his minor role. Whenever Green plays humorously on these underprivileged characters in society, he guarantees laughter, compassion, and recognition, even where the tall tale or broad joke is used. This humorous but loving treatment marks the whole collection of *Salvation on a String*, or characterizes the development of Old Tom in *The Lost Colony*. Cephus enters as a drunkard, a chicken thief, an "Ancient Pistol" in his lies of heroic deeds, and as a lover of Mammy Huzzit, to whom he devotes all his lover's euphemisms so long as she keeps him supplied with food. He functions in a more subtle way, however, when he appears in chains at the very beginning; for his punishment is a mock-heroic comment on the commoner's state. His embarrassing wound in his buttock burlesques the situation in the same way, but, in truth, it was received "mixing too close with a Hessian soldier." And, just as the love affair of Hugh and Eileen parallels that of Thomas and Patty Jefferson, so the marital culmination of Cephus and Mammy Huzzit deepens the factor of love as a healing and binding one in society, particularly in a time of stress.

In all of these affairs Cephus is far more the fox than the fool, for he sees himself as a good reflector of other persons and events. Thus, when his wound draws gibes from the other patients, he turns them away with ease: "The great Thomas Jefferson for one and the same. Ahm, him and me both together are of the same pair alike—downtrodden, spet upon, and misused by the commonwealth of this state." The mocking self-pity disappears as the crisis of the war deepens, and he sheds the man-in-stocks image in his important contribution to the Revolution. Just as Old Tom is reclaimed at Roanoke, so Cephus emerges as part of the "common glory." Fortunately, he does so with a bouyancy and roguery that echo Falstaff's and add enormously to the theme and effect of the play.

As much as in any of these symphonic dramas, the Narrator holds *The Common Glory* together. Dressed like George Wythe —Jefferson's tutor—he sets a believable tone in his description of the sacred spot on which the theater rests. Thereafter, the interaction of the English and the Virginians, vital to a final understanding of the Revolution, is clarified through his explanations. In the same way, he follows each focal scene—except for the Battle of Yorktown which explains itself—as a unifier of the action. He also controls the two projective scenes: the first, in which Jefferson, in "mental speech," writes the Declaration of Independence; the second, the dream sequence already discussed. Altogether, the Narrator, by pulling together the scattered pieces of history, frees the audience for fuller involvement with the personal lives of the characters on the stage. Green considered the role of the Narrator so critical that he gave him the memorable lines of the Declaration of Independence at the end of the play. Later on, as he developed the form of the historic dramas, Green fused the roles of the Narrator and the actors to a greater degree. But, so long as he persisted in this earlier stylistic function of the Narrator, he was nowhere more successful than in *The Common Glory*.

Brooks Atkinson's enthusiasm for *The Common Glory*—"a religious rite, without being pompous or sanctimonious, it serves the American tradition"—was as much for the integration of music as for anything else.[4] Green himself saw the organ in the play as another actor, or as a commentator. His stage directions in the beginning call for chords that suggest "energy, and war and the turmoiling of men's souls and bodies," sounds that lead slowly into wordless harmony. He asks, too, for the organ to produce "a commenting swirl of music." The overture itself sums up the conflict and resulting peace through a subtler combination of the "Veni Creator," a sixteenth-century hymn by J. Farmer; "Hail to the Chief," an old Gaelic melody; and of "Alman," a sixteenth-century virginal piece. The chant by the chorus that follows, "Out of the Rich and Deep-Bosomed Earth," a Henry Purcell song with lyrics by Green, extends the solemnity of the moment and the awesome quality of the spot where "dust and ashes befoul/The bright head of beauty."

The first scene, really a complete one-act play in itself, ends with a second chant by soldiers in the colony, "Here in the Silence of These Hills," a sixteenth-century song that ends appropriately with Green's line, "Hail to thy sons of heroic/Spirit unconquerable!" The music throughout the full two acts, compiled and collected with additional lyrics by Green, sets the mood, springs out of the emotion or action of the moment, and comments subtly on the spoken words. It comprises twenty-nine songs, hymns, ballads, and dance tunes, including The Lord's Prayer from Thomas Estes' sixteenth-century *The Whole Book of Psalms*, which is strategically placed as a prologue to the second act; the lovely lyric attributed to Sir Walter Raleigh, "Now What Is Love," is sung by Patty Jefferson in the tender Christmas scene; the stately dance music of the finale is Handel's "Royal Fireworks Music"; and Green's own composition, "I Took My Gun and Away to War," is sung in fine contrast by Cephus immediately after Jefferson's dream.

As he had effectively demonstrated in the past, Green shows how the historic accuracy and emotional intensity of great men in troubled times can be authenticated in music as well as in words and action. The majestic tone set in the blend of organ, chorus, and the Narrator is sustained throughout the play, lending credibility even to the anachronistic few bars of America's national anthem at the very end.

Although Green concentrated less on the choreography than on the music-integration, the rhythm of the play itself constitutes a flow from crowd to person and back. Thus, in the very beginning, the isolated problem of King George is considered by his court followers, but the subject is lost at once in the carefree dancing. Green implies in their reaction the need for the English to enjoy themselves while the barn burns down. The same superficial situation obtains at Gordon's party until the interruption by Hugh Taylor and his band of rebels.

The contrast of person and crowd can be seen in two successive scenes involving Jefferson: in the first, he feels a desperate loneliness as he composes the Declaration; in the second, he calls the people to the colors in a rousing speech of fellowship. The one and the many are impressed as a fact upon Jefferson himself in the death of his wife and in the death of thousands of others engaged in the pursuit of liberty. Jefferson's fundamental belief in the individual as the absolute unit of society, and of the individual as totally involved in the forming of the corporate personality, is actually dramatized here in the twin roles that Jefferson plays. And, because Green made Jefferson aware of his role as an individual contributing to society and freedom, he was able to leave him less individuated without destroying the dramatic effect. *The Common Glory,* as Cephus intimates, includes all of the people as they progress from slavery to liberty in a new land of equal opportunity. They all appear with great force in Green's first symphonic play on the making of America.

II *Faith of Our Fathers*

The next symphonic drama that Green wrote was his second approach to this subject of the Founding Fathers' engagement in forging a government. The successes at Roanoke and Williamsburg brought Green to national prominence for he was commissioned by the National Capitol Sesquicentennial Commission to celebrate the setting up of the national government in Washington in 1800. He chose as his subject George Washington for a play entitled, *Faith of Our Fathers.* Intended in the planning stages to run for a period of ten years, the play appeared in the summers of 1950 and 1951, but with very little success. Green's memories of the whole period are bitter, beginning with the political roadblocks that were reduced only after President Truman himself intervened, and continuing, as he said, with the nepotism and patronage of "pie counter habitues who had been foisted on our payroll by the yea-saying congressmen and politicians. . . ."

The irony of this failure appears in the enormous outlay of money for the venture, compared with the modest budgets for the previous three symphonic dramas, *The Lost Colony, The Highland Call,* and *The Common Glory.* The huge Carter Barron Amphitheater in Rock Creek Park alone cost almost half a million dollars, as compared to the palatial arena at Williams-

Laying the Foundation of America

burg, which cost only two hundred thousand dollars, or the original one at Roanoke, which did not exceed fifty thousand dollars. Green says that he spent more time soliciting funds to meet these expenses than he did preparing the play, and nothing proves the truth of his assertion more than the unpolished script. To indicate that his was no pose, nor an attempt to foist off blame, *Faith of Our Fathers* remains today one of his few complete but unpublished works.

The play is Green's, however, no matter how much federal bureaucracy substituted for local involvement, or to what degree the author became embroiled in unnecessary production snarls. Even if Green had been freed of the planning, the play to have any worth would have to be radically different from what appeared. Green's work is really only a pageant, one in which Washington epitomizes the American spirit as a vast panorama. Or, if it is drama, the episodic format breaks apart the continuity of action and shatters the progressive illumination of the hero.

After hinting at a probitive search into the sensibility of the big, shy farmer in the first two scenes, Green becomes a historian, presenting external facts in a series of tableaus, or highlighted unconnected episodes. In the first act alone, the events include all of Washington's major decisions from his twenty-seventh year to the founding of the Republic. At this point, the subject of the second act is examined: President George Washington, a man with a new set of hazards and decisions. By this time, the person of Washington has been so abstracted out of the virtues earned in overcoming all of the difficulties of the first act that the audience finds more attraction in the songs and dances than in the fortunes of the hero. Had the author generally observed the unities, as he had intended in the five-day period of the original play, *The Merciless Days*, the dispersion of time and space might have at least been less troublesome. Had he made Washington a man of the soil, as he seemed to intend in the beginning, the stock figure of sentimentality would not have emerged. As it is, *Faith of Our Fathers* stands as a clear failure.

CHAPTER *10*

The Shaking of the Foundation

I *Wilderness Road*

AFTER THE PAINFUL failure of *Faith of Our Fathers*, Green had a dry period of writing. In the same year of 1951, his adaptation of *Peer Gynt* was produced by the Group Theater; in 1953, he brought out *Dramatic Heritage*, a collection of old and new essays; in 1954, he published *This Declaration*, a one-act revision of the Philadelphia scene of *The Common Glory*. Beyond these three works, which added little to his reputation, there was nothing. For an author whose life's energies produced an enormous amount of work, such a span of inactivity is unique. But this period from 1951 to 1955, actually one of latency and reflection, was ended with the appearance of another symphonic drama, in which Green returned to a high level of achievement, in *Wilderness Road* (1955). The subject of the Civil War, violence, peace, and the pursuit of ideals brought him back to material he had previously examined successfully. It allowed him to move with less austere and more identifiable characters through situations and themes that obviously commanded interest.

In the four previous symphonic dramas, Green had been commissioned by a state or local historical association, or by a corporation created for a specific memorial celebration. In 1955, however, Berea College in the hills of Kentucky celebrated its centennial with *Wilderness Road* as its main attraction. The historic struggle for liberty by Berea in an atmosphere of intolerance was ideal for Green. He found in the college's century-old fight for principle a direct historic and philosophic parallel and contrast to the waste and desolation of the Civil War. The play, accordingly, contained the author's larger views on the stupidity of violence and war. These opinions are found everywhere in his writings, but in this play and in *Johnny Johnson* he most forcefully dramatized the inescapable fact that war is a blight on the human scene.

The plot of *Wilderness Road* is very simple. John Freeman, the son of Luke Freeman—a peacemaker killed years ago when he had intervened between feuding parties—returns to the Kentucky hills after three years of enlightened education in Ohio. Like Abe McCranie and Thomas Jefferson, John Freeman's driving efforts to educate his backward people charge the community with enthusiasm, at the same time that the folk are antagonized and threatened by his radical views on democracy; ideas that suggest a sellout to the slick Northerners and the devil. Had the times been more opportune, his ingenuousness and indefatigable drive might have won them over. But his humane appeals coincidentally and naturally echo those of Abraham Lincoln, and they force his friends and neighbors to examine their moral lives where slavery and religious bias constitute a way of life.

Secession by the Southern states opens the breach in the town, with a majority of the people drawn to Jefferson Davis, and a much smaller group loyal to the federal government. When all the young men eagerly join either the Rebel or the Federal forces—including Freeman's young protegé, Neill Sims—John, who continues to hate the sword, exhorts his friends to follow the Bible instead. As the soldiers return home, butchered and mangled by unromantic bullets and shells, John binds their wounds and prays with them, "Rebels and Feds," but he remains adamant in his hatred of war.

When his young friend, Neill, is carried home with a shattered leg, his plaintive cry for his teacher to take up a gun confronts John with the alternatives of fight or retreat. Like the heroes of Green's other plays, the problem is beyond John's solution. The answer, therefore, comes to him in a dream in which his father counsels a course of action that makes John realize that he must enlist at once in the Union Army. His services prove invaluable as a scout, when he leads a battalion in a successful assault on a commanding bridge crucial to Confederate defenses. Through his decisive involvement in this Battle of Perryville, the whole area becomes Union territory; but he is killed in the assault. The play ends with the scattered people once again reunited as a community—ironically, in his funeral cortege—as the Reverend John Fee eulogizes the dead hero.

The whole play works toward this community solidarity but it is achieved only through the lonely efforts and death of the hero. An outsider because he has been gone for three years, John returns to Indian Fort Mountain, where his proposal of Christian education includes black and white, rich and poor, in an equity before unimagined. He infuriates virtually all of the townspeople with his views, so that he is ostracized by the end of the first act. This casting out might have been endurable, except that the girl he loves also joins the group of scorners. The joyful opening of the play hardly prepares him for this acute loneliness that he faces in the completion of his program. The second act, therefore, actually tests the hero's principles.

Even more ironic, the whole play suggests that John's actions precipitate the violence: if he had listened to Jed Willis and the others who advocated the old and tried ways, and "let the niggers be where God intended them," brothers would not be at each other's throats, sweethearts would not mourn their dead lovers, and people would laugh and sing again. This scapegoat role highlights John's centrality in the play in the same way that Hardy Gilchrist and Abe and Will Connelly tragically control the actions of their plays. John returns to the valley with theories of liberty and freedom, but he and they are put to the test. As such, like Socrates and Christ he becomes the Classical "fool of virtue": the idealist destined for death. And only in his death does the community accept him and understand the meaning of his words. A cohesiveness emerges from his sacrifice as the community understands and appreciates how all of his disruptive actions were actually intended for their corporate welfare. In this scapegoat role, John completes the traditional Classical design of harmony resulting from tension, disorder, and the death of the hero.

Nowhere else in his writings has Green so emphasized the alter Christus role of the hero. There are hints of it in Abe and in Gilchrist. Memories of the crucifixion are evoked in the little Negro story, "The Wizzem-oose." Every black prisoner on the chain gang eases the burden of his pick with a hymn to his personal Jesus. But only in this play does Green obviously identify his main character with the larger cause of the nation, then with genuine Christianity, and finally with Christ Himself.

When John first appears, he has been away for a period, like the Christ, readying himself for his people. His dedication to them surprises his girl, Elsie; to her simple mind, once having been outside the mountain, his newer sensibility should make all that he had known before appear repulsive. John's response, instead, is a baptism of the mission he is about to undertake. Fortunately for the drama, he, like Christ, has no understanding of the true nature of the mission: he prays only that he will be ready for whatever comes. And he is quickly put to the test. When hysteria runs high and all the men of the town rush off to war, he remains home to fight for peace. The new leader of the Rebel force in town finds him sawing wood and taking dimensions for the rebuilding of his destroyed school. He scorns John with, ". . . Jesus the carpenter," and thereby continues the exemplar motif. In the critical scene when John has decided to enter the war, a woman screams out, "Merciful Jesus! Jesus!" as Neill's amputated leg drops to the floor.

The dream sequence deepens the Christ image, for it is the voice of the father from above that bolsters the shaky confidence of the son who has now been thrust into a course of violence against his better judgment. This scene had been prepared for on the night before. When the Knights of the White Star—a variant of the Ku Klux Klan—burn his books and rip apart his schoolhouse, he, instead of smashing back, cries out to God that his hate be washed away. Like Christ on the cross, he forgives his enemies in their ignorance. Green also insists on the mockery for the Christ-hero: when John volunteers, a bonnet and a coat are thrust upon him by whores in the camp, as the soldiers and women scream and genuflect in front of him. Another analogue, deliberately slanted, occurs when John delivers his sweetheart into the care of his brother. As the Christ, John forsakes teaching in his school for the more important nursing of the sick. As the Christ, the music that identifies John, "Lonesome Valley," echoes the haunting theme of "Jesus Walked this Lonesome Valley."

All of these scattered, faint and strong allusions are pulled together in John Fee's final eulogy of John Freeman. In it, the preacher praises a noble mission well performed, using as his measure Christ's accomplishment centuries before, and the visionary words of Saint John's Gospel; the two themes combine to complete the hero's role as prophet and martyr. Like Christ then, John walks alone, cutting himself away from sweetheart, mother, brother, and neighbor, until in isolation his hour is fulfilled. His sacrificial death in the attack on the bridge, when every one of his own arguments against war obviated such an action, ironically underscores the harmony of the town at the funeral, and also its ritual aspect. Like Hamlet, misunderstood by the entire court, only in death are John's motives known and his sacrifice gratefully accepted. This alone makes for greatness in the play.

But Green adds a dimension of allegory to the role and the play in other ways. John's early decisiveness leads into a wavering before the vision of his father informs him of the meaning of sacrifice, which, in turn, launches him into equally decisive action and consequent death. Kentucky's position in the Civil War is roughly the same for different characters in the play are torn by the issues that revolve around John. Elsie is more precisely Kentucky, caught between her love for John in peace, for his confusing mystical ideas on union of states and peoples, for his brother Davie in war, and for his clear enthusiasm for local rights and interests. In a very few lines, Green makes Elsie a believable character, even in her allegorical and passive role. Her new love for John upon his return is genuine, but her ideas are the same ones she held years before when he left the valley; for this reason she keeps saying to him, "I don't understand." Had she blindly accepted all of his new ideas, she would have been a fake; for she is like Davie in her limited Confederate sensibility. Accordingly, even though John's death is a personal loss for her, her life with Davie will be a happy one. In her acceptance of the future, she is even more like Kentucky, or like the entire South as it ought to be: the road ahead is to be traveled; the one behind is not be wept over.

Davie, too, is Kentucky; but he represents the state as it felt itself part of the Southern mystique. His ambitions are few and easily realized: a good harvest, a pretty girl who will yield him a few kisses, fun with the boys at a party, "niggers in their place," a man in line when the bugle calls, and all of the other elements that complete a simple personality. But he is also reliable, predictable, loyal, compassionate—he is the one who holds Neill in the brutal surgery; not basically mean, he just sees the truth too late. His mother, Elizabeth, is less clearly a symbol of Kentucky than the sorrowing woman of war; she saw her husband killed in his design for peace, and now sees her two boys fighting on different sides. She is yet another of Green's women who, in the mystery of human suffering, rock from blow to blow.

One otherwise favorable reviewer of the play asked for a more probitive examination of the hero in depth: a flashback to the child John when he sees his father shot dead in the streets; more of a tug of war between his ideal and his obligation, which would introduce dramatic complexity to his final decision; a deeper inquiry into the problem raised by the antihero—why can't John lead a good life as a "live coward," rather than cancel it as a "dead hero"?[1] Green might well have improved the overall effect with a series of flashbacks to establish a firm relationship of father and son.

But the suggestion of the antihero as a solution demands an entirely new character, and a play written by a different author. For if Freeman himself never could entertain such a possibility, he only reflects how everything in Green's life holds repugnant the posture of the antihero. Death as a possible consequence of principled action lies at the basis of Green's philosophy as much as it is integral in Classical tragedy or in Christian ethics. Perhaps Green should have focused on the inner struggle more if the hero was to reflect the *Parable of Modern Times*, as he subtitled his play. But no dramatized struggle could ever detail reasons for and against, in the same way that no computer can present with mathematical precision the forces in the hero's background, the conditions of the present that determine him, and the proper road he must take.

Life defies formula, Green has said over and over again. In this play, he deliberately leaves ambiguous John's confused motive in putting down the Bible and picking up the gun. But so is life complex, and the pursuit of peace is not easily determined. What is clearly demonstrated, even with an obscure motivation, is John's deep sense of loss, however innocuous that loss might appear to an urban, sophisticated person. All of his plans and hopes are in the primitive school and in an education for all children; in the freedom of dissent, which would allow the free thinkers at Berea latitude for their radical programs; in the freedom from harassment, which would shackle the moonlight raids of the Knights of the White Star and other murderous groups. Failing to see these freedoms achieved in his own lifetime, John judges himself inadequate to his mission. But the audience has the benefit of unfolded history or, more immediately, of the tributary scene of the funeral procession which places John's gifts in a larger context of success. This placement properly comes only after a catharsis is effected through the hero's death.

In this play Green traveled a great distance from the dramas about Roanoke and Fayetteville in which he had expressly wished to dramatize the people. His full attention in *Wilderness Road* was on one man who was not the spokesman for his group but who, paradoxically, was more a spokesman than anyone before. The complaint that Brooks Atkinson had over the medium of symphonic drama—its failure to cut vertically into the character's nature—could not apply to John Freeman: for all of the dimensions of music, dance, pantomime, group movement, mental speech, and commentary contributed specifically to the portrayal of Freeman. And, as though Aristotle were proved correct again, in this concentration on the character's development through the plot, Green at the same time synthesized the elements of symphonic drama to greater artistic effect than he had in his four previous dramas, or than he has since. In *Wilderness Road* the Protestant hymnals, the national and local songs, the funny and the tender songs of Appalachia, like "A Frog Went A 'Courtin" and "The Turtle Dove Song"; the simple, spontaneous folk dances and the frenzied mass movements of a people confused by events too big for them to grasp are fused effectively so that subject and form are one. In the intimate eighteen-hundred seat Indian Fort Theater, built out of local stone specifically for this play, Green was able to spread out the panoramic action of the Civil War on the three stages, at the same time that he could close out the large dimension for the closeup scenes vital to genuine drama.

The stature of John Freeman rests to a great degree upon the facts of Kentucky and Berea College. But such a man belongs among drama's great heroes as he images America's pursuit of democracy and as he completes himself on the stage. In *Wilderness Road,* Green achieved the twin effects of historic perspective and dramatic empathy to a degree not found in any of his other music dramas. Despite its brief appearance on the stage, it remains one of the author's major accomplishments.

The Shaking of the Foundation 137

II The Confederacy

Green returned to the subject of the Civil War with *The Confederacy*. When the Tidewater Association of Virginia decided to begin the Civil War Centennial early, it commissioned Green to write a play for the summer of 1958. He deliberately chose the moderate, less colorful figure of Robert E. Lee for his subject, when he might have had more dramatic appeal through the fiery Stonewall Jackson or the cocky Jeb Stewart. Lee, a secular saint in the South, posed no ice-cold figure for him, however, as George Washington had a few years before. Historians, from Lee's own son to Douglas Freeman and Earl Miers, present him as a great American leader, religious and self-confident, but, even more, as a warm, compassionate husband, father, and friend—the very qualities that Green catches in the play. This image transcends regional bounds. Thus, in a Christmas scene Green extracts from history itself when he has Northern soldiers overcome by emotion with Lee's unexpected visit. Also, when he has Northern soldiers line up to touch Lee as he passes at the signing of the treaty, Green does not create a mythical figure as a Southerner would see him but as he was known to all. So Herman Melville found in Lee, particularly in his final hour of ignominy, the sum of human virtue, the classic figure,[2] the same compassionate man Green presents in this symphonic drama.

The play opened on July 1 and continued through the summers of 1958 and 1959, but poor attendance canceled the association's original plans for an unlimited run. Whether the screaming jets over the Robert E. Lee Amphitheater in Virginia Beach shattered the illusion on the stage, or the small community felt a minimum of shrine involvement with Lee, who was hardly connected with the area, or whether the timing, three years before the centennial fever took over the South accounted for the failure is difficult to say.

In approaching his subject, Green wisely chose to see the war only through its impact on Lee, in the same way that he saw the national trauma through Freeman's eyes in *Wilderness Road*. The plot, therefore, is ready-made through the actual involvement of Lee in the battles of the war that led to ultimate defeat of the Confederacy. The story line also takes in the warm domestic life he snatches for moments in Arlington, and a series of temptations he is offered to give up his leadership of the

Southern forces. But in the plotting, Green hewed close to history, seeking to add dimension to his hero through the tragedy of historic event and the choices made in changing situations.

The surest dramatic addition to the five years of history came through the character of William Barrett, an old school chum of Lee's and a spokesman for the North as a successful capitalist. But, aside from the emphasis on individual events and characters, Green emphasized by omission as well. He cut out, for example, the humiliating days after the Battle of Petersburg, when Lee was left surrounded by Sheridan and Grant at Appomatox Court House, left with only seventy-eight hundred of the thirty-five thousand troops he had in the earlier fortification of the Richmond-Petersburg line.

Green faced three major problems in the writing of this play. The first was one of history, like the one he encountered with *The Common Glory*. History has been objectified clearly enough by now so that any person in the North or the South knows of the complex factors of economy, morality, regional prestige, federal union advocacy or states' rights, climate influences, tradition and myth, and all the other elements that combined to bring about the Civil War. The simplistic cry of slavery was adequate as a rallying force when emotions ran high, but it appears now as only one of the factors to the twentieth-century observers who can see, for example, how machinations of the North and the South to build the first transcontinental railroad contributed as much to bring on the war. Even with this distance in time, however, the 1861 debacle still evokes an emotional response with a flag unfurled, a song sung, or a vignette told about the war dead. This was a built-in problem that Green faced. Conscious of the pitfalls involved in the production, his selection of Lee, his own restraint, deep feeling, and fairness balanced the subject matter so that *The Confederacy* rises above regional pride in its dramatic effect.[3]

A second problem was the proper exposition of the issues of the war without blurring the image of the hero or breaking the forward movement of the play. In the previous symphonic plays, Green had used the stylized narrator as the cohesive agent, whose presence at the beginning and end of each scene was expected by the audience. But with *Wilderness Road,* and the dramas that followed, he fused the narrator, chorus, and actors as integral parts of the action. The Narrator in this play serves as an army chaplain, reminds the viewers of the hallowed place and sacred past, casts the events back into history, and also returns occasionally to fill in other required facts. But he functions more as the chaplain, ministering to the wounded, conducting services for the dead, and simply moving through the tragic period of history as another Virginian.

Thus, instead of utilizing the narrator and the chorus to explicate the background, Green presents the actions themselves, and the characters whose postures represent opposing views. Barrett, accordingly, represents the North when he speaks, just as Jefferson Davis, Alexander Hamilton Stephens, and Judah Benjamin present the Southern point of view. As such, their respective arguments with Lee disclose the differences that separate the North and the South, and those that divide Lee and the other Southern advocates. In this way, Green not only disclosed the necessary historic facts, but also uncovered aspects of Lee's character which endeared him to the audience.

A third problem faced the playwright in the writing of this play: the staging of the many battle scenes and other contributory ones that involved Lee. To solve it, Green selected certain battles for dramatic explication: Petersburg instead of Gettysburg and the second Battle of Richmond instead of the Wilderness. He then used Expressionistic devices to establish the facts and atmosphere of war. Much of the action was a projection through Lee's eyes as the general watched from a distant hill. His barking commands to his officers and his comments on the fighting were complemented by thundering sounds and flashing lights and racing couriers on and off the hill. Instead of simulating a battle on the stage, Green had the flags of the Blue and Gray fight symbolically. In place of the tragic mistake that caused Jackson's death at Chancellorville, he captured the event and the first major hint of the lost cause in a funeral procession of great pageantry.

Jackson's death is a high point of the play, one dramatized in terms of failure rather than in the triumph his troops achieved in battle. The choice Green made here is consistent with history; but, even more, it adds a poignancy to the loss the romantic Confederates were about to suffer. The sweep of the fire through the South is captured in the marching songs familiar to everyone, music which becomes another actor through repetition and varied commentary. The anguish of all the people—North and South—

comes out in the nostalgic songs, as it does in the playlet scenes when the separate nations prepare for war, and, later, when they care for their sick and dead. Green also used skrims to create the illusions he needed. In fact, he used every theatrical device to impress the thunder and violence of war without blunting his audience into insensibility. The swift movement; the shifting musical sounds, from "We are coming, Father Abraham," to "Dixie," and "O, Lord of Hosts"; the heated dialogues brought on by the temper of war; the ideals of the hero shunted aside for duty—all become a unified effect in the ringing bells at the end of the play, sounding a new life for Lee at Washington College.

The Confederacy was Green's second and last symphonic drama on the Civil War. Unlike *The Highland Call* and *Faith of Our Fathers,* it is a good play. The worst that can be said of it is that a few loose ends in the second act could either be dropped or tied in more effectively. In it, of course, it was necessary to include more of the war than in *Wilderness Road,* or than would be of great interest to contemporary viewers.

In each play, Green's attention, as it has been throughout his life, is on the man and not on the event. Although neither Freeman nor Lee successfully swerves the immediate direction of history, each man's action under pressure produces, paradoxically, the community harmony traditionally found in Classical tragedy. Green seems to say through the two men that no matter how great the travail, and how obvious the defeat, the hero refuses to collapse. In his enduring courage, he sets the tone for human behavior so that life is a little better because of his having lived as he did. If there are no other marked differences between the early and the later Paul Green, this emphasis on heroic conversion of a moment in history, a kind of hallowing the everyday, typifies the Green from the 1950's on.

CHAPTER *11*

New Areas for Exploration

I *The Stephen Foster Story*

THE SUCCESS of the symphonic dramas for Paul Green and for his accomplished colleagues—Kermit Hunter, Lynn Riggs, Ramsey Yelvington, Emmet Lavery, and others—rests on a universal sense of the past as much as on any other factor. Daniel Boone, General Custer, Paul Revere, and Thomas Jefferson are figures of history and myth with ready-made dramatic achievements waiting to be plotted on a stage. The plays, added to every year, compose, in turn, an Idea of Theater—a theater connected intimately with the people by reason of the dramatic material and through a psychological readiness for history. Green demonstrated in the eight plays already discussed how history comes alive, not only in the re-creation of these great heroes, but even more in the presentation of them as normal, everyday folk troubled and gladdened by shifting events and impulses. Jefferson's honest admission of a loss of faith in democracy, for all of his theories, and General Lee's gentle attention to his crippled wife, when the Confederate Army was in shreds, bring these men out of the stale pages of history as vibrant human beings. As much as he found potential drama in these national figures, however, Green invariably included in his plays the lesser lights, the common men and women buried in the anonymity of the past. Dan Murchison, John Rolfe, and even Buck McIntosh in *The Confederacy* contribute to the making of America as expressions of a working democracy that includes the great and the small.

In the last three symphonic plays on the making of America, Green eschewed the heroic achievements of the past and went directly to the heart of the people, through the songs they sing and love, in *The Stephen Foster Story*, through pioneer extension of the nation's borders into new states, in *Texas*, and through the Moravian mission of Christianity to the Indians in Ohio, under the inspired leadership of David Ziesburger, in *Trumpet in the Land*. These plays are incidentally connected with the Civil War, but they are particularly concerned with the indigenous American culture found in its little people. The dramas continue in the successful symphonic form; but, like the experience of *Wilderness Road*, they indicate the new subject areas waiting to be explored and also demonstrate Green's flexibility: his continued willingness to invent and to explore all of the resources of theater.

In *The Stephen Foster Story*, Green returned to the hills of Kentucky, specifically to Bardstown and to the site of the Federal Mansion, traditionally connected with Foster's, "My Old Kentucky Home." He returned, too, to the folk material of his earlier writings; for in Stephen's Foster's melodies he dealt with America's first authentic folk songs. The Forty-Niners sang "Oh! Susanna" in their treks across the gold fields of California, until it became the state's best-known song. "Uncle Ned," also published in 1848, spread beyond America's borders and achieved international fame within the year. There were other writers of songs before him, but Foster was the first to find his inspiration and themes in America rather than in Europe. He was the first to blend successfully a sentimental melody with familiar idiom, so that people hummed, danced, and tapped their feet to real American music.

All of the action of *The Stephen Foster Story* is located in and around Pittsburg, except for one major scene toward the end of Act I, when Stephen visits Old Federal Hill on a business trip, and where legend has him writing "My Old Kentucky Home." In addition to this unity of plot, Green chose one year—1848-49—to tell the story; and he telescoped the years as though all of the music was written during this period.[1] Meticulous in observing historic fact and implication in his other plays, Green decided to observe only the general facts of the hero's life and to transmit an over-all impression consonant with the music. Accordingly, he saw no need to introduce any of the sordid events connected with the poverty, drink, and despair of the Bowery years before Foster's death in the Bellevue Hospital in his thirty-seventh year. The gay, wonderful music called for a happy ending, one with Stephen winning his Jeannie with the light brown hair and with the two sailing away on the Allegheny River for new heights in New York City.

This ending fits in with the rest of the play: like the hero's mercurial ways, the rhythm of events is up and down. Thus, although he obviously can have Jane's love for the asking, Stephen is cast out because of his Bohemian life. But, when down in fortune, he receives a great chance to prove himself in a business deal, only to lose it because of drinking and listening to a Southern belle's flattery. All this while, his spirits are buoyed up by whiskey, and he finally realizes he is a drunkard. The up-and-down movement anticipates the actual conclusion that could have been written after the final curtain, after the romantic departure for New York.

Foster as a dreamer follows other Green characters. Danny, in *The Laughing Pioneer*, the *No 'Count Boy*, and some of the wilder ones in the Bethel County stories suggest that life is too short for a man to be buried under economic and domestic problems. Stephen tries to interest himself in his father's failing business and in the mounting debts. He determines that he will do a first-rate job for Mr. Igoe on the trip to Federal Hill. He convinces himself that he will settle down and earn the right to marry Jane. But the dreams drive all of the promises out of his mind as he tries to capture the melodies he hears in his head. Somehow, the joy of dancing around with the maid, Lievey, as they sing "Nelly Bly," seems more important than learning bank procedures. Such contrasts of personality and ways of life constitute the plot of the play, or the development of Stephen's relationships in Pittsburgh.

But the plot is more of an excuse to frame Foster's compositions than to search out the inner dynamics of the man. There is no growing up in dreamers like him: there is only the punishment inflicted by society, or the reward of joyous adulation. Accordingly, the play depends more on stage effects than any other play that Green wrote to this time, for everything must remain on the surface. The music, of course, dominates the play, with all of Foster's songs dramatized, but with all of them secondary to "My Old Kentucky Home." The dances and general group activity are effectively spun off the music, like the techniques used in the more artistic musical comedies that followed the lead of *Oklahoma*. Green fused the music and dance so well that they filled out the characters' outlines, so that a Narrator was not required to inform the audience. This fact alone suggests how far away Green moved from the form of *The Lost Colony*.

This play contains all of the romantic and sentimental elements that would guarantee immediate failure at a Broadway box office. Despite this, the drama has succeeded in its large, open-air theater, attracting large audiences. This thin line between sentiment and sentimentality was one Green had risked many times before. In *The Stephen Foster Story* he managed to fuse the man and his music into a believable character in depth; one with sensitivity to nature and people, but one confused by what he feels compelled to do and by what society expects of him. His influence on all those around him implies that, notwithstanding his dreamy impracticality, Stephen is loved precisely, if secretly, because he is the free soul in a society that demands conformity. Because everyone loves his hero, despite obvious faults, Green brought all of the people together in a happy ending, as they sing Foster's most famous song. All of the gaiety of the people in laughter, the tender quality of the songs, and the ingenuousness of Foster disclose for a few hours the joy that emerges from simple folk art. In *The Stephen Foster Story*, Green made his hero and the songs he wrote a single piece.

II Texas

Six years after the opening of *The Stephen Foster Story*, Green went to an even more remote section of the country to write his next symphonic drama. He called the play *Texas*, and in the title he indicated the broad subject he would cover and the effects he hoped to achieve. The play has been an extraordinary success in the four seasons since 1966, although it had a slow start in the first two weeks. But the local Texas enthusiasm for "their" play is not shared by those who see Paul Green as second only to Eugene O'Neill in America for his dramas *In Abraham's Bosom*, *The House of Connelly*, and *The Hymn to the Rising Sun*, or as an eminent writer of prose in the stories of *Salvation on a String* and in the novel *This Body the Earth*.

Green sets the tone of *Texas* from the outset: the spectacular will achieve an end that no script could improve upon. As the

New Areas for Exploration

darkness comes on, high above on the canyon cliff a lone rider, silhouetted against the sky, sounds on a trumpet the first two phrases of "Oh, Bury Me Not on the Lone Prairie." A beam of light picks him up in the distance as the call is repeated: it then fades in the thunder of beating hoofs. "Turkey in the Straw" music follows the beating sounds, giving way in turn to a group of six flag bearers, five carrying the five flags of Texas, and the sixth the Stars and Stripes. So the play moves back and forth through the lonesome, the festival, and the majestic until the grand finale completes the spectacle. The production attests to the vision and direction of William and Margaret Moore and to the choreography of Neil Hess. But it also regrettably shows Green's willingness to have his play upstaged by nature. The overwhelming impression in *Texas* comes from the setting of the Pioneer Amphitheater. Fifteen thousand acres comprise this gorged-out cleft that runs one hundred and twenty miles, in an area southwest of Amarillo, the very heart of the "uninhabitable" Panhandle. The theater itself is a feat of engineering, but the esthetic effects of the six-hundred-foot backdrop and the overhead blanket of stars achieve an impression of enclosure in the huge outdoors that is nature's achievement. The illusion of depth at the Lake Matoaka Amphitheater in Williamsburg is complementary to the script of *The Common Glory,* just as the intimacy of the Berea College theater contributed to the theme explored in *Wilderness Road.* But nature in Palo Duro Canyon State Park completes itself; or, if it is incomplete, only a Lear in his naked madness, or an Oedipus enraged in self-hate, could be its fitting counterpart. Instead, cowboys, Indians, and farmers engage in petty quarrels; sing songs like "Clementine," "Silver Threads Among the Gold," and "Home on the Range"; and throw themselves into wild hoe-down dances and plum-picking parties against this terrifying scene. Without question, such prosaic pursuits did occupy the lives of these early pioneers in western Texas, but the placement of them in design against the artistry of the cliffs and sky reminds one of Horace's words about the mountain and the mouse.

This is not to suggest that caricatures of Texas itself, or the Hollywood version of the Texan buckaroo, rendered the subject matter trite from the outset. On the contrary, the cowboy who mixed gentlemanly codes with a cavalier swagger and who punched longhorns, fought prairie fires, and built delicate windmills to eke out precious water in a drought-ridden land constitutes one of our finest mythical figures. But Uncle Henry, Dave Newberry, and the other cowboys in this play talk their hardships and dance their woes; at no time do they fill out the legendary role in dramatic action.

Despite the historic facts and framing, and Green's sure sense of theater, *Texas* remains only a light entertainment. For two hours, the familiar, time-tested songs and dances are rehearsed. One-dimensional characters proceed through predictable situations to solutions of no significance. The thunder, lightning, and canopy of stars have no counterpart in the issues pursued on the stage. Like the awesome setting, the things of nature overpower the tiny people performing there.

CHAPTER *12*

Conclusion

THIS STUDY SHOULD end perhaps with a discussion of symphonic drama, inasmuch as Green devoted thirty years of his career to this form. Green's own esthetic judgment on this genre literally shifted the direction of his writing away from a style and subjects that had brought him a different kind of success. As a result, despite the many common grounds of ideas and expression, literary historians should note the existence of two Paul Greens: one, the first-rate author of folk literature; the other, the innovator of successful outdoor drama. Therefore, a final word must be said of each.

I *Folk Literature*

Time will probably secure the reputation of the Paul Green of folk literature as a major literary figure. From the earliest experiments with the one-act play in his years at the university through the powerful explorations of heroes in full dramas and novels, he moved with insight and craft to a high level of achievement. The first eighteen years of his life on his father's farm served as an apprenticeship for art that left an indelible mark. The land, as a result, permeates and cloys, pleases and destroys, and fills out the scene of his plays and stories as an extension of man. *This Body the Earth*, for example, summarizes the many Green works in which a man is faced against the forces of nature that test the strength of his character.

In seemingly simple, straightforward narration of the lives of little people who are swallowed up in the great events of history, Green brought the tools of social science to his compassionate examinations of Abraham McCranie, Hardy Gilchrist, and all the others connected with the soil. Thus, one theme of identity crisis persists through this early writing, particularly as it concerns the Negro. The white man has his own major difficulty resisting the loss of self through absorption into the soil, or through submersion by a Southern family and tradition. Will Connelly's tragedy develops precisely out of this predicament. But the black man, to a far greater degree in these writings, has no clue as to who he is or where he fits in. Like Faulkner's Joe Christmas, in *Light in August,* he meekly accepts an image handed him by the white man, or ironically, by other blacks. Because the Negro has no part in the shaping of this image, he attempts to flesh it out in conformity with directions, until he discovers that it is really a mask that resists growth and change. The fine one-act plays, *A Start in Life* and *Hymn to the Rising Sun,* detail poignantly this black man's circumscribed existence, the foolishness of rage upon the discovery, and the sad fact of man's inhumanity to man.

At the same time, this social concern and psychological probing disappear in the greater artistic emphasis on the divine potentiality in every human being. Like Walt Whitman before him, Green refuses to condemn humanity for its ills, although war, religious and race bias, economic inequities, and greed discourage optimism. Instead, he sees mankind as "forever growing," as slipping slightly with each new step forward, but as reaching toward an apotheosis. This defined perfectionism determines his concept of tragedy. Like the Greeks, he exposes the hero to the realities of existence; he plunges him close to the bottom of despair until capitulation or destruction spells out the end. At this low point, the hero refuses to be destroyed and asserts his victory in defeat. This challenge and response pattern of Classical tragedy constitutes the greatness of *In Abraham's Bosom* and *The Field God.* It defines man in his ordinary actions, which have in them, paradoxically, the extraordinary possibility of transcendence.

II *Symphonic Drama*

Notwithstanding this artistic achievement, Green turned toward a different literary expression in 1937. *The Lost Colony* marked this shift that brought the artist to a popular success he had not really enjoyed before. The ten symphonic dramas that followed, and the numerous others by his colleagues, clearly demonstrate that the form is now a permanent part of the American scene. The dramas also anticipate the possibility of more refined and effective plays in the future. Regardless of the box-office popularity, however, the fact remains that the very character of the form demands a subversion of the creative imagination for literary effects. The substance of drama, ancient or modern, lies in plot, character, thought and diction, woven into a single effect of empathy. This effect arrives as an illusion of reality created in a tight relationship of act and agent, of word and act, and of characters and background. The concession to the verisimilitude takes the audience into the author's consciousness and to the mysterious profit that rewards this whole process of imitation. But the form of symphonic drama raises the least of drama's elements to a priority that nullifies the search for character: spectacle tends to destroy plot line and character development.

Green, however, argues otherwise in numerous essays on the outdoor theater. He insists that the form in no way subverts the true function of drama, anymore than the Kabuki's stylized pantomime, or the Aeschylean ritual effects, cancel out the life and theme of the play. Yet he admits in his long essay on the development of the symphonic drama that his involvement is more that of a coordinator, or a leader of an orchestra. As such, the word at most is only a part of the many media of music, dance, group movement, pantomime, and the other elements that comprise spectacle. The reader—removed from the theater and equipped only with the text and the author's stage directions—can only imagine or hope that the fusion of all the parts does produce an effective whole. But the words on the page, the substance of literature, fail to move him.

The radical shift by Green in 1937 did not produce a totally new author. Thus, his uncanny sense for human motivation and lyric expression persisted and enabled him to maintain a plot line and character identification that the spectacle at all times threatened to overcome. Obviously, the play's new form explored dramatic possibilities for him that the indoor framed stage denied. Placing one hundred and fifty actors on a stage at once, for example, allowed him choreographed patterns that were possibly as vocal as any phrasing he could invent. Three stages on many different planes, with props supplied by lakes, trees, sky, and wind expanded the imagination to cosmic proportions.

The enthusiastic response of over three and a half million people who have seen *The Lost Colony* alone, suggests that the medium touched a sensitive nerve in the country. It surely served notice that the stranglehold that commercial theater has wielded can no longer be exerted. In 1967, for example, American National Theater and Academy sponsored a symposium in New York to examine the meaning and future of this medium in America. One contribution that the outdoor drama makes, aside from the artistic merits of each play, is bringing the theater to millions of people who would otherwise never see anything outside the movies. Green himself, in the Cape Fear Valley, never saw a play prior to his freshman year at Chapel Hill. Through greater availability, in turn, the subject matter which springs out of a national heritage prepares the way for younger artists to create in a milieu that approximates Francis Fergusson's Idea of an American Theater: the meeting of the playwright and the audience through the play that becomes an actual ritual experience.

Green observed only recently that this role of precursor or preparer might be cited as the sum of his contribution: "No, I don't think symphonic drama must necessarily find its best expression or servitors in the South. But I do think that what some of us have been able to accomplish is still forerunning work; I think often of that brave spirit I used to know, Percy MacKaye, and his huge masques. He, too, was a forerunner. Maybe after us all will come an Aeschylus, a Sophocles, a Euripedes. Maybe not, I have hope."[1] If the future does hold an American Aeschylus, the symphonic drama will indeed lead to an indigenous American theater and to praise of Paul Green as its founder.

III Now and Hereafter

After all these years, Green continues to write and to grow in his profession. In December, 1968, he allowed the North Carolina Folklore Society to publish *Words and Ways,* containing stories and incidents from his Cape Fear Valley Folklore Collection. This is only a small part of a voluminous work, *Home to My Valley,* to be published in 1971. For three days in March, 1969, his "Folk Morality Fantasy," *Sing All a Green Willow* was presented by the Carolina Playmakers at Chapel Hill. Green wrote it as a Fiftieth Anniversary gift to this Carolina group that still remains a vital part of him.

In the summer of 1970, in Dover, Ohio, Green's symphonic drama, *Trumpet in the Land*, was produced in a new amphitheater constructed specifically for this play. The "Trumpet" is David Ziesburger, leader of the Moravian missionaries in Ohio.[2] Green has also completed another symphonic drama, *The Golden Isle*, to be produced in 1972. It has to do with the robber-baron period, particularly with those powerful, rich men who set up their little baronies on Jekyll Island, just off the Georgian coast. The state of Georgia has appropriated a half million dollars for the venture, which includes the digging of a lake as background for the huge stage.

There are other outdoor dramas waiting for him to write, Green believes, including one on Sam Houston in Texas, and one on George Rogers Clark in Kentucky. He thinks now and then of the Pilgrims off Cape Cod, and of the Christian missionaries in California. A stronger possibility for production seems to be a play on Washington, D.C. Abraham Lincoln, certain members of Congress, a few Negro leaders, like Frederick Douglass and Sojourner Truth, would be involved in the difficulties that developed immediately after the Civil War, when great numbers of black people flocked into Washington. Green sees the subject matter as a timely parallel to the events in the summer of 1968, when the Poor People's Campaign climaxed its enormous difficulties in Washington.

There seems to be no end to this prolific author's imaginative grasp of history as charged material for drama. The course he set for himself in 1937, not clearly marked at the time he wrote *The Lost Colony*, has taken him into wide sections of the American scene, where he has tapped the springs of greatness in America's past and present. Moreover, he continued in these epic plays the substance of his folk literature; a confidence in the resiliency of human nature under the severest tests, and a belief that the common man and the democratic process are the stuff of great literature.

Notes and References

Chapter One
1. These fictional single and married women can be documented in Margaret Hagood, *Mothers of the South: Portraiture of the White Tenant Farm Woman* (Chapel Hill, 1939).

Chapter Two
1. Paul Green, "Folk Drama Defined," *The Carolina Playbook,* III (June, 1939), 54.
2. Despite an otherwise favorable review, John Mason Brown saw the last two scenes as unrelated to the previous action of the play: *Saturday Review of Literature,* XIII (July 2, 1927), 40-41. Brooks Atkinson considered the play as "obviously overwritten," although certain scenes evidenced an imaginative power, dramatically realized: "Field God," *New York Times* (April 22, 1927), 18. Joseph Wood Krutch found no flaws at all, as he judged the play superior to Eugene O'Neill's *Desire Under the Elms:* "Folk-tragedy," *The Nation,* CXXIV (May 4, 1927), 510-511.
3. Paul Green, *Dramatic Heritage* (New York, 1953), p. 82.
4. Robert Penn Warren, "Some Recent Novels," *The Southern Review,* I (1935-36), 642-45.
5. Howard Mumford Jones, "This Body the Earth," *Saturday Review of Literature,* XIII (November 30, 1935), 12.

Chapter Three
1. Agatha Boyd Adams, *Paul Green of Chapel Hill* (Chapel Hill, 1951).
2. John Gassner, ed. *Five Plays of the South* (New York, 1967), ix.
3. Winifred Dusenberry, *Loneliness in American Drama* (Gainsville, Florida, 1960), p. 151.
4. Stark Young, "Shadow of Wings," *New Republic,* LXVIII (October 14, 1931), 234-36.
5. The two plays are obviously alike, even to specific incidents repeated. When the dinner gong sounds out like a lamentation over the Connellys' death, it echoes the plucked string of the Russian

past. Will's offer of five hundred dollars for the sale of his boxwood parallels Lyubov's bid for the cherry orchard. In both plays, the ball in the midst of poverty expresses a gesture of futility.

6. This ambivalence constituted the play's greatness, according to Joseph Wood Krutch: "A Promise Fulfilled," *The Nation*, CXXXIII (October 14, 1931), 408.

7. Robert Cantwell, "The Laughing Pioneer," *New York Herald Tribune* (September 11, 1932), 6.

8. Maristan Chapman, "A Tale of the Southland," *Saturday Review of Literature*, IX (September 24, 1932), 124.

9. Barrett Clark, *Paul Green* (New York, 1928), p. 10.

10. Stanley Young, "The Life of the Southern People in Dramatic Form," *New York Times*, Section VI, 15. (June 11, 1939).

Chapter Four

1. Seymour L. Gross, "Stereotype to Archetype," *Images of the Negro in American Literature*, ed. S. L. Gross and T. E. Hardy (Chicago, 1966), p. 3.

2. The first published collection contained one Negro play: *The Lord's Will and Other Carolina Plays* (1925). *Lonesome Road, Six Plays for the Negro Theater* appeared in the following year. In 1928, *In the Valley and Other Carolina Plays* included eleven plays, six of them on the Negro. The Negro appeared in the short stories even earlier: four of them in 1924, in *Salvation on A String*. Seven more were included in *Dog on the Sun* (1949). Four other one-act plays and three other dramas appeared over the years as separate publications. I will treat them as overall Negro thematic material, rather than in connection with a specific publication, or in chronology.

3. John Gassner had a higher regard for the play. He included it in *Twenty-Five Best Plays for the Modern American Theater* (Early Series) (New York, 1935).

4. Green's authentic touch seems verified in the same dramatic crisis told by Green's good friend, James Weldon Johnson: *The Autobiography of an Ex-Colored Man* (New York, 1965), Chapter III.

5. "I have since learned that this ability to laugh heartily is, in part, the salvation of the American Negro; it does much to keep him from going the way of the Indian." Johnson, p. 56.

6. Barrett Clark, Introduction, *Lonesome Road* (New York, 1926), p. xii.

7. Kenneth Macgowan, Hatcher Hughes, and Bennett Kilpack

thought otherwise. They awarded the play first prize in a competition organized by La Petit Theatre du Vieux Carre of New Orleans: Edith Isaacs, "The Tributary Theater," *Theater Arts Monthly*, XI (May, 1927), 390.

8. The original story, in *Salvation on A String*, "The First Death," involved white characters. Both versions are substantially the same.

9. Frederick Koch, "The Negro Theater Advancing," *The Carolina Playbook*, VI (September, 1933), 101-2.

10. Brooks Atkinson, "Ten Free Authors," *New York Times* (May 25, 1941), Section X, 9.

Chapter Five

1. Brooks Atkinson, "Folk Drama of the South," *New York Times* (February 20, 1927), Section X, 1.

2. Percy Hammond, "The New Prize Play," *The Literary Digest*, XCIII (May 28, 1927), 47.

3. George Goldsmith, "*Abraham's Bosom*, at Provincetown, is Tragedy of the South," *New York Herald Tribune* (December 31, 1926), 10.

4. John Mason Brown, "Frontiers in the Theater," *Saturday Review of Literature*, III (March, 1927), 170.

5. This is taken up in a fine study of Green's theology, by Woodrow Geir, "Images of Man in Five American Dramatists: A Theological Critique," Unpublished Ph.D. thesis (Vanderbilt University, 1959).

6. When Paul Robeson saw the play, he asked Green where he had picked up one of the songs; he had never heard it before, but it surely was Negro. Green replied, "Oh, that one, no, I wrote that myself, I reckon." Clark, *Green*, p. 9.

7. Clark, *Green*, p. 14.

8. R. Dana Skinner, "The Pulitzer Prize Play," *Commonweal*, VI (May 25, 1927), 74.

9. Joseph Wood Krutch, *The American Drama Since 1918* (New York, 1957), pp. 247-48.

10. Hallie Flanagan, *Arena* (New York, 1940), p. 200.

11. Both quotes are from Green's letter to Miss Constance Webb (May 9, 1967): copy in my files.

12. Ernest Starr, "Paul Green's *Native Son*," *Winston-Salem Journal-Sentinel* (April 27, 1941), 10.

13. Richard Wright, "How Bigger Was Born," *Saturday Review of Literature*, XXII (June 1, 1940), 14.

Notes and References

14. Brooks Atkinson, "*Native Son,*" *New York Times* (April 6, 1941), Section X, 1.
15. "Paul Green's *Native Son,*" *North Carolina Anvil* (May 21, 1967), 4.

Chapter Six

1. Green's delight with the Kabuki, which he discovered on his 1952 tour of the Orient, only confirmed these early concepts of drama.
2. Barrett Clark, "Tread the Green Grass," *New York Times* (July 24, 1932), 46.
3. R. W. Gordon, "Old Songs Traced to the Mountains," *New York Times* (January 9, 1927), 7, 17.
4. W. David Sievers, *Freud on Broadway* (New York, 1955), p. 318. He saw the play as brilliantly conceived and original in its symbolism, even though its Freudian overtones strain the limits of theater. He calls it one of the most original and powerful works of the imagination by an American playwright.
5. Brooks Atkinson, "Experiment in Epic Drama," *New York Times* (October 14, 1934), Section X, 1.
6. W. P. Eaton, "Prize Plays and Authors," *New York Herald Tribune* (May 19, 1935), 11.
7. Edith Isaacs, "Roll, Sweet Chariot," *Theater Arts Monthly*, XVIII (November, 1934), 814.
8. It had a fairly successful run at the Provincetown Playhouse in 1941 in a new production by the Popular Theater.
9. W. P. Eaton, "Five Plays in Print," *New York Herald Tribune* (May 9, 1937), 31.
10. Robert Benchley, "Johnny Johnson," *Literary Digest*, CXXIII (January 21, 1937), 23.
11. Stark Young, "Mr. Collins and Johnny," *New Republic*, LXXXIX (December 9, 1936), 179.

Chapter Seven

1. *Wilderness Road*, based on fiction, and *The Confederacy*, in which Lee has no connection with Virginia Beach, are the exceptions.
2. George McCalmon, Christian Moe, *Creating Historical Drama* (Carbondale, Illinois, 1965), p. 9.
3. Allen Tate, "Last Days of the Charming Lady," *The Nation*, CXXI (October 28, 1925), 485-86.
4. The carol is one of Green's favorite pieces. For him, it evokes the simple personal emotion at the same time that it produces a com-

monalty through liturgy.

5. Brooks Atkinson, "Founding Fathers," *New York Times* (August 15, 1937), Section X, 1, 2.

Chapter Eight

1. An account of the historical MacDonald family can be found in Dorothy Quynn, "Flora MacDonald in History," *North Carolina Historical Review*, XVIII (July, 1941), 236-58.

2. *The Founders* continued there through the summers of 1957 and 1958, but then moved over to the Lake Matoaka Amphitheater in 1964.

3. Brooks Atkinson, "Founding Fathers," *New York Times* (August 15, 1937), Section X, 1, 2.

Chapter Nine

1. This does not include an adaptation of *Peer Gynt* for the Group Theater in 1951.

2. In 1947, the first scene was actually a series of pantomimes depicting the preparation for war. It was cut in the second season.

3. This scene that reads so well played poorly. Green cut it in production.

4. Brooks Atkinson, "Virginia's Glory," *New York Times* (July 27, 1947), Section II, 2.

Chapter Ten

1. Henry Hewes, "Optimism Under the Pines," *Saturday Review of Literature*, XXXIX (August 4, 1956), 30-31.

2. Herman Melville, "Lee in the Capitol," *Collected Poems*, ed. Howard P. Vincent (Chicago, 1947), 145-52.

3. Lewis Funke, "History Relived," *New York Times* (July 13, 1958), Section II, 1.

Chapter Eleven

1. *Beautiful Dreamer*, for example, written by Foster only a few days before his death, is sung here at the end of the play.

Chapter Twelve

1. Letter to this writer (May 13, 1967): copy in my files.

2. *Trumpet in the Land* was produced too late for me to include any discussion here.

Selected Bibliography

PRIMARY SOURCES

Many of these plays, stories, and essays appeared in periodicals and anthologies. I have listed the best and most available editions. There is no definitive collection.

Salvation on A String. New York: Harper, 1924.

Contemporary American Literature (In collaboration with Elizabeth Lay Green). Chapel Hill: University of North Carolina Press, 1925.

The Lord's Will and Other Carolina Plays. New York: Holt, 1925. Contains: *The Lord's Will, Blackbeard* (In collaboration with Elizabeth Lay Green), *Old Wash Lucas, The No 'Count Boy, The Old Man of Edenton, The Last of the Lowries.*

Lonesome Road: Six Plays for the Negro Theater. New York: Robert M. McBride Co., 1926. Contains: *In Abraham's Bosom* (one-act), *White Dresses, The Hot Iron, The Prayer Meeting, The End of the Row, Your Fiery Furnace.*

The Field God and In Abraham's Bosom. New York: Robert M. McBride Co., 1927.

In the Valley and Other Carolina Plays. New York: Samuel French, 1928. Contains: *In the Valley, Quare Medicine, Supper for the Dead, Saturday Night, The Man Who Died at Twelve O'Clock, Unto Such Glory, The Man on the House, The Picnic, In Aunt Mahaly's Cabin, The Goodby, The No 'Count Boy.*

Wide Fields. New York: Robert M. McBride Co., 1928.

The House of Connelly and Other Plays. New York: Samuel French, 1931. Contains: *The House of Connelly, Potter's Field, Tread the Green Grass.*

The Laughing Pioneer. New York: Robert M. McBride Co., 1932.

Fixin's (In collaboration with Erma Green). New York: Samuel French, 1934.

This Body the Earth. New York: Harper, 1935.

Shroud My Body Down. Iowa City: Clio Press, 1935.

Johnny Johnson. New York: Samuel French, 1937.

The Lost Colony. Chapel Hill: University of North Carolina Press, 1937.
The Southern Cross. New York: Samuel French, 1938.
The Lost Colony Song-Book. New York: Carl Fischer, 1938.
The Critical Year. New York: Samuel French, 1939.
Franklin and the King. New York: Dramatists' Play Service, 1939.
Out of the South (Fifteen plays revised). New York: Harper, 1939.
The Enchanted Maze. New York: Samuel French, 1939.
Native Son (In collaboration with Richard Wright). New York: Harper, 1941.
The Highland Call. Chapel Hill: University of North Carolina Press, 1941 (Includes *The Song-Book*).
A Start in Life. The Free Company Presents. ed. James Boyd. New York: Dodd, Mead and Co., 1941.
The Hawthorne Tree. Chapel Hill: University of North Carolina Press, 1943.
Forever Growing. Chapel Hill: University of North Carolina Press, 1945.
Song of the Wilderness (Music by Charles Vardell). Chapel Hill: University of North Carolina Press, 1947.
The Common Glory. Chapel Hill: University of North Carolina Press, 1948.
Dog on the Sun. Chapel Hill: University of North Carolina Press, 1949.
Peer Gynt (Adaptation). New York: Samuel French, 1951.
The Common Glory Song-Book. New York: Carl Fischer, 1951.
Dramatic Heritage. New York: Samuel French, 1953.
Wilderness Road. New York: Samuel French, 1956.
The Founders. New York: Samuel French, 1957.
Drama and the Weather. New York: Samuel French, 1958.
The Confederacy. New York: Samuel French, 1959.
Wings For To Fly: Three Plays of Negro Life. New York: Samuel French, 1959.
The Stephen Foster Story. New York: Samuel French, 1960.
Five Plays of the South (Five plays revised). ed. John Gassner. New York: Hill and Wang, 1963.
Plough and Furrow. New York: Samuel French, 1963.
Cross and Sword. New York: Samuel French, 1966.
Texas. New York: Samuel French, 1967.
Texas Song-Book. New York: Samuel French, 1967.
Words and Ways. North Carolina Folklore. XVI (December, 1968).
Home to My Valley. Chapel Hill: Univ. of No. Carolina Press, 1971

Selected Bibliography

SECONDARY SOURCES

ADAMS, AGATHA BOYD, *Paul Green of Chapel Hill.* Chapel Hill: University of North Carolina Press, 1951. Profile of author's life through 1950.

ATKINSON, BROOKS. "South of Times Square," *The Carolina Playbook,* I (September, 1928), 10-13. See also *New York Times* (February 20, 1927), Section X, 1; (October 14, 1934), Section X, 1; (August 15, 1937), Section X, 1, 2; (April 6, 1941), Section X, 1; (May 25, 1941), Section X, 9. One of the earliest discoverers of a "great lyric poet," his reviews praise the dramas prior to 1937 and reserve judgment on the symphonic dramas.

BROWN, JOHN MASON. *Upstage.* New York: W. W. Norton, 1930, pp. 40-50. See also "Frontiers in the Theater," *Saturday Review of Literature,* XIII (March 8, 1927), 170; "Plays and Works," *Saturday Review of Literature,* XIII (July 2, 1927), 940-41. Sees author as theatrically awkward but one of the finest lyric poets in America, because of the intense presence of God and man in all of his work.

CARMER, CARL. "Paul Green, the Making of An American Dratist." *Theater Arts Monthly,* XVI (December, 1932), 995-1006. Observes how subjective material results in a great play like *In Abraham's Bosom,* whereas objective distance, such as in *The House of Connelly,* leads to failure.

CARROLL, WALTER. "Playwright as Believer," *Theater Arts Monthly,* XXXVII (July, 1954), 53-55. A good account of the growth of outdoor drama in the United States.

CHAPMAN, MARISTAN. "A Tale of the Southland," *Saturday Review of Literature,* IX (September 24, 1932), 123-24. Sees the author of the novels as an authentic poet of the soil.

CLARK, BARRETT. *Paul Green.* New York: Robert M. McBride Co., 1928.

——. Introduction, *Lonesome Road.* New York: Robert M. McBride Co., 1926.

——. "Notes on Paul Green," *Drama,* XVI (January, 1926), 137, 155; *New York Times* (May 9, 1927), 7, 17. Rare praise for a poet who speaks as a white man or a black man with the same authority.

CLARK, EMILY. *Innocence Abroad.* New York: Alfred Knopf, 1931.

Includes a profile of Green's life in Harnett County, during the early years.

DUSENBERRY, WINIFRED. *Loneliness in American Drama.* Gainesville: University of Florida Press, 1960. Sensitive study of twentieth-century man searching for relationships, as expressed on the American stage.

EATON, WALTER P. *The Drama in English.* New York: Charles Scribners, 1930. See also "American Drama," *New York Times Magazine* (February 19, 1928), 6-7, 20; *Books* (May 19, 1935), 2; *Books* (May 9, 1937), 31; *Books* (July 9, 1937), 2; *Books* (July 23, 1939), 2. Sees rare talent demonstrated in the short stories, novels, and one-act plays but not in the dramas where discipline is needed for tighter form. Even so, Green might do for the South what Lady Gregory and Synge accomplished for Ireland.

FERGUSSON, FRANCIS. "Out of the South," *Southern Review,* V (Winter, 1940), 565-66. Praises this genuine, poetic voice of the South.

FLANAGAN, HALLIE. *Arena.* New York: Sloan, Pierce & Co., 1940. Numerous allusions to the part Green played in the Federal Theater Project, and to the government involvement in a few of his plays.

FUNKE, LEWIS. "History Relived," *New York Times* (July 13, 1958), Section II, 1. Despite the pageant aura in his symphonic dramas, admires how Green successfully fuses characters, themes, and action.

GASSNER, JOHN. Introduction. *Five Plays of the South.* New York: Hill and Wang, 1963.

―――. "Broadway in Review," *Educational Theater Journal,* V (October, 1953), 236-37. Sees him as an original poet with daring experimentation that may lead to a new kind of American theater.

GEIR, WOODROW. "Images of Man in Five American Dramatists: A Theological Critique," Unpublished Ph.D. thesis (Vanderbilt University, 1959). Notes how all of the writings express a fundamental belief in the unity and transcendence of man and in the uniqueness of man as responsible to his neighbor and to God. They also indicate how Green has always been haunted by the ideal of perfection.

GREGORY, MONTGOMERY. "The No 'Count Boy," *Opportunity,* III (April, 1925), 22. Sees in Green that rare white man sensitive to the language and sensibility of the black man: this should point the way to a new appreciation of the black culture.

HEWES, HENRY. "Playwright as Believer," *Saturday Review of Literature*, XXXVII (July 10, 1954), 24; "Optimism Under the Pines," *Saturday Review of Literature*, XXXVIII (August 4, 1956), 30-31. An intense political religion of democracy gives Green's work a dimension lacking in other contemporary dramatists.

ISAACS, EDITH. *The Negro in American Theater*. New York: Theatre Arts, 1947.

―――. "Roll, Sweet Chariot," *Theater Arts Monthly*, XVIII November, 1934), 813-14; "Paul Green, A Case in Point," *Theater Arts Monthly*, XXV (July, 1941), 488-98. Unabashedly theatrical, Green has raised Tributary Theater to a high level. No one, except for O'Neill, has a better chance of writing the great American drama.

JONES, HOWARD MUMFORD. "Paul Green," *Southwest Review*, XIV (Autumn, 1928), 1-8; "Two Carolina Novels," *Saturday Review of Literature*, XIII (November 30, 1935), 12. Sees a new Whitman emerging, a mystic, the lyric poet of the soil.

KRUTCH, JOSEPH WOOD. "A Promise Fulfilled," *The Nation*, CXXXIII (October 14, 1931), 408; "Fool of God," *The Nation*, CXLIII (December 5, 1936), 674-76. Generally sympathetic to this new lyric voice in drama, he is cautious because of structural awkwardness in the plays.

LOCKE, ALAIN. "The Drama of Negro Life," *Theater Arts Monthly*, X (October, 1926), 701-6. Green speaks for a new South, enlightened in political, social, and literary views.

LOWER, CHARLES and WILLIAM FEE. *History into Drama*. New York: Odyssey, 1963. Case book on *The Lost Colony*.

MALONE, ANDREW E. "An American Folk Dramatist," *The Dublin Magazine*, IV (April, June, 1929), 31-47. He judges Green and Synge as one in achieving lyric effects in drama. *In Abraham's Bosom* is the most significant play of our time.

McCALMON, GEORGE and CHRISTIAN MOE. *Creating Historical Drama*. Carbondale: University of Southern Illinois Press, 1965. Comprehensive account of outdoor drama in America, including all of Green's, except the last four.

MEADE, J. R. "Paul Green," *Bookman*, LXXIV (January, 1932), 3-7. Extraordinary praise of Green as one of the best on the American scene.

OWENS, H. G. "The Social Thought and Criticism of Paul Green,"

Unpublished Ph.D. thesis (New York University, 1945). Lists all of the social problems raised in Green's plays.

POUPEYE, CAMILLE. "Un Ecrivain Pour le Théatre Nègre en Amérique: Paul Green," *La Renaissance D'Occident*, XIX (1926), 195-202. What O'Neill is for the North, Green is for the South. General introduction of Green to the French reader.

RABKIN, GERALD. *Drama and Commitment*. Bloomington: University of Indiana Press, 1964. Enormous talent and genuine social involvement found in the early plays thrown away for showy pageants.

SELDEN, SAMUEL. *Frederick Henry Koch*. Chapel Hill: University of North Carolina Press, 1954. Traces Koch's influence on Green.

SIEVERS, W. DAVID. *Freud on Broadway*. New York: Hermitage House, 1955. *Tread the Green Grass* is one of the most original and powerful works of an American playwright.

TOBIN, JAMES E. "Southern Drama, New Style," *Commonweal*, VI (July 27, 1927), 296-98. Eugene O'Neill, Padraic Column, and Green are the poets of the little people of society, dramatically captured in beauty and cruelty side by side.

TREAT, DONALD R. "Paul Green's Concept of Symphonic Drama and Its Application to His Outdoor Plays," Unpublished Ph.D. thesis (University of Denver, 1963). Highly informative on the facts of the symphonic dramas, with an essay on the differences between the pageant and the symphonic drama.

WARREN, ROBERT PENN. "Some Recent Novels," *The Southern Review*, I (1935-36), 642-45. Green writes with the authentic touch of a man who has tilled the soil, cursed it, and praised it in lyric poetry.

YOUNG, STARK. "Mr. Collins and Johnny," *New Republic*, LXXXIX (December 9, 1936), 179; *New York Times* (June 11, 1939), 15. As a fellow Southerner, appreciates the authentic expression of a dramatic poet, but is generally unsympathetic because of sentimentality and theatrical awkwardness.

Index

Index

Adams, Agatha Boyd, 24
Adding Machine, The (Rice), 65
Aeschylus, 150
Aiken, Conrad, 96
America: the building of, 120-29; European colonization, 98-119
American Dilemma, An (Myrdal), 66
American Heritage, 94
American National Theater and Academy, 150
American Regionalism (Odum and Moore), 66
Anastasia State Park (Florida), 115
And They Shall Not Die (Wexley), 66
Anderson, Maxwell, 56, 66; *What Price Glory?*, 88
Anderson, Sherwood, 56
"Archie and Angus," 10-11
Aristotle, 136
Atkinson, Brooks, 59-60, 83, 102, 114, 126, 136
Aunt Mahaly's Cabin (one-act play), 50-51

Baker, George Pierce, 107
Belasco Cup award, 55, 59
Bell, Albert, 98
Benét, Stephen Vincent, 56
Berea College, Kentucky, 130, 136, 145
Berlin Opera, 78, 80
Berlin theater, 77
Bethel County stories, 10, 19, 25, 35, 108, 120, 143
Bibliography, 157-162
Black folk-literature, 39-58; attempted escape, 43-56; daydreams, 53-55; "Frizzle," 43, 50; *The Hot Iron*, 41-43; "How Grandma Found Her Love," 43; *The No 'Count Boy*, 53-55; redemptive suffering, 41-43; religion and superstition, 49-53; sadness and tragedy, 40; *A Start in Life*, 56-58;
treatment of black man, 48-49
Blue Thunder, 50
Boone, Daniel, 141
Borden, John, 100, 102-3, 105, 111, 114
Boyd, James, 56
Brass Check, The (Sinclair), 21
Brecht, Berthold, 77, 83, 93
Brown, John Mason, 60
Bryant, Farris, 115
Buies Creek Academy, 1
Burns, Haydon, 115
Bury the Dead (Shaw), 88

Caldwell, Erskine, 12; *Tobacco Road*, 66
Cambell, James, 1
Cape Fear Valley, 108-9; Folklore Collection, 150
Carolina Playmakers (Chapel Hill), 53, 59, 86, 99, 108, 150-51
Carter Barron Amphitheater (Washington, D. C.), 128
"Chair Endowed," 6
Chapel Hill, 80, 86, 88, 150
Chekhov, Anton, 33-34; *The Cherry Orchard*, 33-34
Chlumberg, Hans, 88
Civil War, 130-36; *The Confederacy*, 137-40; *Wilderness Road*, 130-36
Civil War Centennial, 137
Clark, Barret, 26, 80
Clark, George Rogers, 151
Clurman, Harold, 36
Common Glory, The, 97, 111, 120-28, 138, 145; historic context, 122-24; music and choreography, 126-28; narrator, role of, 126; themes and characters, 121-29
Confederacy, The, 97, 137-40, 142; historic context, 137-39; music, 139-40; story line, 137-38; themes and characters, 137-40
Connelly, Marc, 56
Conrad, Joseph, 7, 13

Control: A Pageant of Engineering Progress (Baker), 107
"Cornshucking, The," 8
Cort Theater (NYC), 13, 82
Cove Amphitheater (Williamsburg), 111-12
Crawford, Cheryl, 26, 87
Cross and Sword, 97, 114; dance and group movements, 118; historic contest, 114-16; music, 117; themes and characters, 114-19
Custer, General George A., 141

Dawn's Early Light (Lavery), 96
Declaration of Independence, 122, 124, 126, 128
Desire Under the Elms (O'Neill), 33
Dett, R. N., 53
"Devil's Instrument, The," 10
Dog on the Sun, 108
Douglass, Frederick, 151
Dover, Ohio, 151
"Dr. Hyde," 11
Dramatic Heritage, 130
Dreiser, Theodore, 72
Duberman, Martin, 96

Eaton, W. P., 83, 89
Eliot, T. S., 96
Enchanted Maze, The, 108
End of the Row, The, 44-47, 58
Epic dramas, 93-94; *see also* Symphonic dramas
Ethan Frome (Wharton), 13, 15
European colonization of America, 98-119
European theater, 77-80
Experimental Group, 26
Expressionist devices, 31, 82, 139

Faith of Our Fathers, 97, 111, 128-30, 140
Family and tradition, 24-38, 57
Farrell, James, 66
Faulkner, William, 39
Light in August, 148
Federal Theater Project, 99
Fergusson, Francis, 150
Field God, The, 12-18, 24, 38, 77, 81, 87, 93, 104, 121, 148; critical reaction, 27; failure of, 13; plot line, 13-18; production of, 13; versions of, 17-18
Fine Wagon (one-act play), 57
Fixin's, 5
Fletcher, John Gould, 96
Folk drama, 1, 12
Folk literature, 147-48; *see also* Black folk-literature; White folk-literature
"Folk Morality Fantasy," 150
Forever This Land (Hunter), 96
Foster, Stephen, 95, 142-44
Founders, The, 97, 111, 118, 121; music, 112; themes and characters, 110-14
"Free Company Presents: A Collection of Plays about the Meaning of America, The," 56
Freeman, Douglas, 137
"Frizzle," 43, 50

Garrick Theater (NYC), 59
God and religion, 2, 9-11
Golden Isle, The, 151
Goldsmith, George, 60
Gone With the Wind (Mitchell), 94
Good Soldier Schweik, The (Hasek), 88
Goodbye, The, 46, 58
Gothic plays, 50, 52
Granowsky, Alexis, 77, 83, 93
Grapes of Wrath, The (Steinbeck), 66
Green, Irma, 5
Green, Paul: compassion for humanity, 37-38, 56, 73, 148; editor of *The Reviewer* 59; Guggenheim Fellowship, 77, 78, 120; musical influences, 79; social concern, 24, 65-66, 147-48; symphonic dramas, 148-50; themes, 1-11; world travel, 77, 120
Greenwich Village Theater (NYC), 13, 59, 80
Greville, Sir Richard, 100
Group Theater, 87, 130
Guggenheim Fellowship, 77, 78, 120

Index

Hammond, Percy, 60
Hardy, Thomas, 7, 21
Hasek, Jaroslav, 88
Hawthorne, Nathaniel, 7, 96
"Her Birthday," 5-6, 36
Heroes, folk, 2, 13, 148; Christus role, 132-34; classical tragic, 64; moral heroism, 45-47
Hess, Neil, 145
Hickerson, Harold, 66
Highland Call, The, 97, 111, 118, 119, 121, 125, 128, 140; Scottish songs and ballads, 109-10; themes and characters, 108-110
Historic dramas, 92-98
Hitler, Adolph, 90
Home to My Valley, 150
Hoover, Gladys, 96
Hot Iron, The (one-act play), 41-43
House of Connelly, The, 26-34, 35, 38, 93, 144, 148; ending changed, 32-33; production of, 26, 32; themes and characters, 27-34
Houston, Sam, 151
"How Grandma Found Her Love," 43
Howard, Sidney, 107
"Humble Ones, The," 9
Hunter, Kermit, 96, 141
Hymn to the Rising Sun (one-act play), 65-68, 69, 72, 93, 144, 148; mood-thesis, 66-68

Ibsen, Henrick, 12, 93, 130
In Abraham's Bosom (one-act play), 60
In Abraham's Bosom, 13, 47, 71, 72, 73, 77, 93, 121, 144, 148; awarded Pulitzer Prize, 59-60; critical reaction, 26-27, 59-60, 64; production of, 59; themes and characters, 60-65
In the Valley (one-act play), 82
In the Valley and Other Carolina Plays, 3, 25, 48, 49, 50, 82, 85
In White America (Duberman), 96
Indian Fort Theater (Kentucky), 136
Irish playwrights, 2
Isaacs, Edith, 83
Jackson, Stonewall, 137

Jamestown, Virginia, 111
Jamestown Corporation, 121-122
Jefferson, Thomas, 121-128, 131, 141
Jekyll Island, Georgia, 151
Job, 4, 7, 14, 18, 42
Johnny Johnson, 79, 92, 93, 131; critical reaction, 90, 94; themes and characters, 87-91
Jungle, The (Sinclair), 21

Kierkegaard, Sören, 64
Kipling, Rudyard, 58
Koch, Frederick, 1-2, 37, 52, 77-78, 79, 85, 95, 98; adviser to *Lost Colony*, 99; *Raleigh, The Shepherd of the Ocean*, 98, 107
Krutch, Joseph Wood, 94

Lafayette Opera House, 108
Lake Matoaka Amphitheater (Williamsburg), 121, 145
Last of the Lowries, The (one-act play), 6
Laughing Pioneer, The, 24, 35-38, 93, 143; narrative structure, 37; themes and characters, 35-38
Lavery, Emmet, 96, 141
Lawson, John Howard, 65
Lee, Canada, 69
Lee, Robert E., 137-140, 141
Lee Amphitheater (Virginia Beach), 137
Lexington (Howard), 107
Lincoln, Abraham, 64, 131, 151
Lindbergh, Charles, 71
Lonesome Road: Six Plays for the Negro Theater, 3, 44-47, 48
Lord's Will and Other Carolina Plays, 3, 9-10
Lost Colony, The, 78, 93, 97, 98-108, 110, 111, 114, 118, 120, 121, 125, 128, 144, 148, 150, 151; attendance, 99; critical reaction, 102, 114; form and structure, 97; music, 101, 104-5; production, 98-99; prologue, 104-5; themes and characters, 99-106
Lumpkin, Grace, 21

MacDonald family, 108-110
Mackaye, Percy, 107, 150

MacLeish, Archibald, 56
Majestic Theater (NYC), 69
Man on the House, The (one-act play), 85
Man Who Died at Twelve O'Clock, The (one-act play), 52
Man's Reach (Hoover), 96
Marching! Marching! (Weatherwax), 21
Martin Beck Theater (NYC), 26
Melville, Herman, 7, 137
Menendez De Aviles, Pedro, 115-18
Merciless Days, The, 129
Mercury Production, 69
Meredith, Burgess, 56
Miers, Earl, 137
Miracle at Verdun (Chlumberg), 88
Mitchell, Margaret, 94
Modern Language Association, 96
Moore, Harry E., 66
Moore, William and Margaret, 145
Music dramas, 78-79; see also Symphonic dramas
Myrdal, Gunnar, 66
Narrators, 126; function of, 138-39
National Capitol Sesquicentennial Commission, 128
National Committee for the Defense of Political Prisoners, 72
Native Son (adaptation for stage), 40, 66, 69-73, 108; form and structure, 71; themes and characters, 66-73
Negroes, 38, 39-58, 59-73, 148; compassion for, 39-40, 148; superstitions, 51-53; see also Black folk-literature
New York theater, 77
No 'Count Boy, The (one-act play), 53-55, 59, 73, 143
North Carolina Folklore Society, 150
Northwest Passage (Roberts), 94
Notes and references, 152-156

O'Connor, Flannery, 96
Odum, Howard W., 66
Oenslager, Donald, 88
Oklahoma, 144
Old Man of Edenton, The (one-act play), 7
Old Wash Lucas (one-act play), 4-5

O'Neill, Eugene, 26, 33, 85, 144
Oregon Centennial, 96
Out of the South, 17, 32, 38
Outdoor theater, 95, 96, 149-50; see also Symphonic dramas

Pageants, 107
Palo Duro Canyon State Park (Texas), 145
Peace on Earth (Maltz and Sklar), 88
Peer Gynt (adaptation), 12, 93, 130
People's theater, 99
Picnic, The (one-act play), 13, 24, 31; themes and characters, 25-26
Pilgrims, 151
Pioneer Amphitheater, 145
Pirandello, Luigi, 88
Pocahontas, 112-14
Potter's Field, 82, 104
Prayer Meeting, The, 48
Processional (Lawson), 65
Proletarian novel, 12, 21
Provincetown Players, 59
Pulitzer Prize awards, 13, 59-60, 80, 83, 93
Purcell, Henry, 127

Rabelais, 38
Raleigh, Sir Walter, 98, 99, 111, 127
Raleigh, The Shepherd of the Ocean (Koch), 98, 107
Regional theater, 59
Return of Buck Gavin, The (Wolfe), 12
Revere, Paul, 141
Reviewer, The 59
Rice, Elmer, 65
Riders to the Sea (Synge), 6
Riggs, Lynn, 96, 141
Roanoke Historical Association, 98
Roanoke Island and the Lost Colony, 98; see also *Lost Colony, The*
Roberts, Kenneth, 94
Roger Bloomer (Lawson), 65
Rolfe, John, 112-14, 141
Roll, Sweet Chariot, 79; critical reaction, 83; themes and characters, 82-85
Roosevelt, Franklin D., 99
Roosevelt, Theodore, 90

Sacco-Vanzetti case, 66
St. Augustine, Florida, 114
St. Francis of Assisi, 89, 90
St. James Theater (NYC), 69
Salvation on A String (collection of short stories), 1, 3, 8, 10, 11, 38, 43, 93, 125, 144
"Salvation on a String," 10
Sam Tucker (one-act play), 60
Saroyan, William, 56
Saturday Night (one-act play), 3, 8
Scottsboro case, 66, 72-73
Selden, Samuel, 85-86, 87, 88, 98
Shakespeare, William: *King Lear*, 12, 125; *Macbeth*, 92; *Othello*, 10, 70
Shaw, Irwin, 88
Sherwood, Robert, 56
Shrine drama, 110; see also Symphonic dramas
Shroud My Body Down, 55, 79, 85-88; mood and atmosphere, 86; themes and characters, 86-88
Sign for Cain, The (Lumpkin), 21
Sinclair, Upton, 21
Sing All a Green Willow, 150-51
"Sixth of June, The," 8-9
Smith, John, 112
Sophocles, 12
Southern Cross, The (one-act play for radio), 13, 24; themes and characters, 34-35
Southern settings, 27-28, 34, 39, 95-96
Spanish dominance in Florida, 114
Start in Life, A, 56-58, 73, 148
Steinbeck, John, 66
Stephen Foster Story, The, 142-44; music and dance, 142-44; plot and characters, 142-45
Stevens, Thomas Wood, 107
Stewart, Jeb, 137
Strasberg, Lee, 26
Street Scene (Rice), 65
Strindberg, August, 85
Stringfield, Lamar, 80, 85, 87, 99, 101
Sullivan, Walter, 96
"Sun Go Down," 57
Supper for the Dead, 51
Symphonic dramas, 79, 147, 148-50; about forging a government, 97; audience involvement, 78, 90, 94; *The Common Glory*, 97, 120-28; *The Confederacy*, 97, 137-40; *Cross and Sword*, 97, 114-16; experiments in new form, 77-91; explorations of the New World, 97; *Faith of Our Fathers*, 97, 128-30, 140; *The Founders*, 97, 110-14; *The Highland Call*, 97, 108-10; history and drama, 92-98; *Johnny Johnson*, 87-91; *The Lost Colony*, 91, 98-106; *Roll, Sweet Chariot*, 82-85; *Shroud My Body Down*, 85-88; *Texas*, 97, 144-46; *Tread the Green Grass*, 80-82; *Trumpet in the Land*, 97; *Wilderness Road*, 97, 130
Synge, John Millington, 6

Tate, Allen, 96
"Tempered Fellow, A," 3-4
Tenant farmers, 3-4, 35, 37, 41, 59
Texas, 97, 142, 144-46; music and choreography, 145-46
Theater Arts (periodical), 83
Theater Guild, 26, 59
Themes, 1-11; black folk literature, 40-41; God and religion, 2, 9-11; land and soil, 1-11, 23, 24; love and mutuality, 2, 6-9; nature's hostility, 2, 3-6
This Body the Earth (novel), 1, 19-23, 24, 93, 144, 147; pattern of tragic failure, 22-23; sociological ideas, 21; themes and characters, 19-23
This Declaration (one-act play), 130
Tidewater Association of Virginia, 137
Tobacco Road (Caldwell), 66
Toward the Western Sky (Riggs), 96
Tread the Green Grass: A Folk Fantasy in Two Parts with Interludes, Music, Dumb Show and Cinema, 55, 79, 80-82, 86, 90; theatrical problems, 81; themes and characters, 80-82
Tributary Theater, 93
Truman, Harry S, 128

Trumpet in the Land, 97, 142, 151
Truth, Sojourner, 151

United Nations, 120
University of Iowa, 80
University of North Carolina, 1
Unto Such Glory (one-act play), 10
Utopia, (More), 99

Vardell, Charles, 109-10
Virginia, Pageant of, 107
Virginia Beach Amphitheater, 137
Virginia Company, 111

Warren, Robert Penn, 21
Washington, George, 128-29, 137
Washington, D. C., 128, 151
Waterside Theater, 99, 108
Weatherwax, Clara, 21
Weill, Kurt, 87-88, 89, 91
Welles, Orson, 56, 69
West End Yiddish Theater, 77
Westminister Choir, 99
Wexley, John, 66
Wharton, Edith, 13-15
What Price Glory? (Anderson and Stallings), 88
White, Gov. John, 100
White Dresses (one-act play), 40, 43-48, 73
White-folk Literature, 12-38; *The Field God,* 12-18, 24; *The House of Connelly,* 12, 24, 26-34; *The Laughing Pioneer,* 12-13, 24; *The Picnic* (one-act play), 13; *The Southern Cross,* 13; themes, 40; *This Body the Earth,* 19-23, 13, 24
Whitman, Walt, 2, 16, 95, 118-19, 148
Wide Fields, 3
Wilderness Road, 97, 111, 137, 138, 140, 142, 145; allegories, 134; Christus role of the hero, 132-34; music and dance, 133, 136; plot, 131-32; themes and characters, 130-36
Williams, Horace, 1
Williamsburg, Virginia, 111, 121-22; Cove Amphitheater, 111-12; Lake Matoaka Amphitheater, 129, 145
Wilson, Woodrow, 88
"Wissem-oose, The," 132
Wolfe, Thomas, 12
Words and Ways, 150
Wright, Richard, 40, 66, 69

Yelvington, Ramsey, 141
Young, Stark, 33, 90, 94
Your Fiery Furnace (one-act-play), 47, 48, 60

Ziesburger, David, 142, 151
Zimmerman, L. I., 118